Will You Ever Be Rich?

Best Kept Secrets of the World's Richest People

Victor Lofinmakin

THE CORNERSTONE PUBLISHING

WILL YOU EVER BE RICH?

Copyright © 2022 by **Victor Lofinmakin**

Paperback ISBN: 978-1-957809-01-4

eBook ISBN: 978-1-957809-02-1

Printed in the United States of America. All rights reserved solely by the author. This book or parts thereof may not be reproduced in any form, stored in a retrieval system, or transmitted in any form by any means—electronic, mechanical, photocopy.

Published by:

Cornerstone Publishing
A Division of Cornerstone Creativity Group LLC
Info@thecornerstonepublishers.com
www.thecornerstonepublishers.com

Author's Contact

To book Victor Lofinmakin to speak at your next event or to order bulk copies of this book please use information below:

victor@victorlofinmakin.com | +1 832.788.1782
www.victorlofinmakin.com

FOREWORD

I feel very much honored and humbled to have been called upon to write the foreword to this marvelous manuscript.

When Victor Lofinmakin first asked me to write this piece, my response was, "You know I'm a pastor. I cannot endorse anything that's in any way contradictory to the scriptures."

Victor is a shining example of entrepreneurial excellence and administrative astuteness. We have partnered together on multiple business projects and I've always been astounded and astonished at his impeccable integrity, outstanding communicative skills and infectiously vivacious spirit.

Now, I must admit that if this book was authored by me, it would have contained multiple scriptural quotations. But please don't be fooled; the principles expatiated here are in sound alignment with the Bible, and if practiced by anyone, anywhere, will bring the individual to a place of financial freedom.

Like the force of gravity, these are principles that govern life and living, regardless of religious convictions. It's a must-read for Christians and non-Christians alike.

Dr. Ayo A. Ajim

DEDICATION

This book is dedicated firstly to my family; my ever-loving wife, Dolly Lofinmakin - without her, none of this would be a reality; my beautiful kids, Jade, Dola and Jimi Lofinmakin; my parents and siblings - thank you for all the encouragement and support; my extended family, cousins, in-laws, friends, employees, clients, colleagues, mentors and all. Indeed, this book is dedicated to everyone that has come into my life and enriched it in one way or the other.

ACKNOWLEDGMENTS

I want to acknowledge my parents for the amazing job they did in raising me. I was a particularly stubborn child and I am sure it took the absolute grace of God for them to have given me a solid upbringing.

Special thanks to my accountability partners that pushed me so hard to finish this book, Segun Ogungbemi and Lana Bamiro

I want to acknowledge my high school (secondary school), Lagos State Model College, Meiran, Lagos State, Nigeria, for providing us with a strong educational foundation for academia and for life.

I want to acknowledge Nigeria - the country in which I was raised, until my late teenage years - for providing me with critical training in the school of "hard knocks".

I want to acknowledge the United States Navy, for perhaps being the most influential institution in my career. The mentors, the lessons, the discipline and so many more benefits that have enriched my life through my 19 years and counting in the United States Navy have been invaluable.

I want to acknowledge the people in my real estate career - mentors, leaders, employees, clients, and thousands of other people that I have encountered in this wonderful career. You all have made this possible.

Thank you.

PREFACE

As most of my readers may already know, I had published two books prior to this. I titled them "Success Made Simple" and "Finding Happiness Is Your Purpose".

This latest release, "Will You Ever Be Rich?", has a unique focus. It is not about success, happiness or a balanced life. It is about just one thing: Getting rich. It is about making tons and tons of legitimate cash in record time.

I have chosen Oliver as the central character of this piece, and we shall be exploring the chronicle of his journey from the depths of financial struggles to the heights of financial comfort. The ultimate goal is to discover the strategies for amassing and maximizing wealth, just as he did.

As you apply the principles that we will be unravelling at each stage of Oliver's transformation, you will be inspired to take strategic steps towards growing your finances to unprecedented dimensions and enjoying unlimited financial freedom!

Contents

Foreword..5

Dedication...7

Acknowledgments...8

Preface...9

1. What's Your Number?......................................13
2. How Do You Define Rich?...............................21
3. The Path To Riches...29
4. Best Secret Of The Rich....................................31
5. Producers Versus Consumers............................49
6. Boosting Your Odds Of Getting Rich...............61
7. Creating A Solid Spending Plan.......................71
8. Homeownership And Retirement Accounts.....81
9. Debt And Wealth-Building...............................89
10. Investing And Compound Interest...................101
11. Quick Steps To Wealth-Building......................109
12. Where To Invest...129

Conclusion...145

References...147

1
WHAT'S YOUR NUMBER?

"Your economic security does not lie in your job; it lies in your own power to produce—to think, to learn, to create, to adapt. That's true financial independence. It's not having wealth; it's having the power to produce wealth."

– Stephen Covey

Oliver wasn't quite the average Joe - at least, in his mind. He was sure he had an above average intellect. Even though he procrastinated often, he saw himself as having a positive and decent attitude to life. He read often and believed he was going to be successful and famous. Lately, though, he had begun to have this gnawing feeling of dissatisfaction within. He was about to turn 28 and he just felt that his life wasn't really turning out the way he would have wanted it.

On the eve of his 28th birthday, Oliver went out for a run. He loved to exercise outdoors, walking or running. He usually had his best flashes of inspiration while out there getting the dry breeze of Phoenix, Arizona, on his face.

Oliver reflected as he ran. Despite his talents and education, life had dealt him cards that he didn't really like. Not exactly bad cards, but not what he wanted either. By the way, he had a stable job, which fetched him a low six-figure salary. He also had a very supportive wife – Scarlett – who worked and brought home high five figures. They had a son, Sammy, and Scarlett was five months pregnant with their daughter. Despite her domestic duties and the pregnancy, Scarlett still managed to pull a full shift as a nurse.

Thinking through it all, Oliver could not help being perplexed. Despite his family's income, which was approximately 3.5 times the national average and which - according to the Census Bureau's report on Income and Poverty in the United States - put him at above 95 percent of all Americans, he still didn't have the financial freedom he craved.

Oliver felt he was just barely keeping his head above water. For instance, he could not afford to go on a vacation for six months (not that he wanted to, but having the ability to take a vacation for six months or more was something he desired). After factoring taxes, mortgage, car payments, utilities, insurance of all kinds, HOA, and the rest, he barely had enough for emergencies and savings. He found this extremely disappointing, as he had done everything he considered necessary to attain the American Dream. He had gone to a good school, gotten a good job, and was a decent saver, to name a few.

Enter Benjamin

After his run, Oliver decided to pay a visit to Benjamin. Benjamin was his brother-in-law, whose life journey had obviously followed a more enviable path than Oliver's.

Benjamin had retired from full-time employment at the age of 42, to manage his vast real estate portfolio, which spread across Arizona. He had several millions in his bank accounts. He was perhaps the richest person Oliver knew one-on-one.

Benjamin spent one week in a month on vacation. He attended all the premier sporting events, no matter where it was held. He and his family attended the World Cup tournament every four years, as well as the Summer Olympics. They could afford to travel around the world, as they had investments that funded their lifestyle.

Oliver decided to have a talk with Benjamin and ask him about the formula for being rich. He rang up Benjamin soon after and asked if he could pay him a visit sometime during the weekend. Benjamin agreed to a visit but said he would prefer it to be on Tuesday at 2 pm. This, he said, was because he would be taking his family to Trinidad from Thursday to Monday to enjoy the Spring Carnival. He added, by the way, that Trinidad had the best carnivals, despite all the hype about Brazil.

Oliver was not so disposed to a weekday visit, since he had to work Monday through Friday. But maybe he could find a way to make it work. He asked Benjamin if they could meet before 9 am. He could push off getting to work a little late and blame the hectic Phoenix traffic. That was easier than having to leave the office at 2 pm to drive to the affluent, acreage suburbs where Benjamin lived. That was about a 47minutes drive from the hustle and bustle downtown where Oliver worked.

Benjamin declined the suggestion, explaining that his mornings were precious to him. He cherished the luxury of his mornings so much that he never used an alarm clock. In fact, he despised them; they made him feel like he was under the gun. He woke up when his body chose to. Thereafter, he went to his backyard, which had a beautiful pool with a gorgeous waterfall. There was also a standard tennis court and an outdoor lake with a paddleboat. The beautiful scenery often refreshed and inspired him for the day's activities. While there, he would crank up his surround sound system to his favorite jazz station, while he read for about 30 minutes. He would then proceed to take a 20-minute run to his local gym, where he would work out for 40 minutes and then took another 20 minutes to run back. He never picked up his phone until 10 am, at the earliest.

Oliver was fascinated by Benjamin's meticulous morning routine. It was the exact opposite of his. In fact, he had zero control over his schedule. He couldn't decline or cancel any meeting as he wasn't in control of any. His time was owned by others and he was fully committed to doing their biddings.

Determined to see Benjamin on that same Tuesday, the only option left for Oliver was to take a day off work (unpaid) as he had exhausted his paid time off (PTO). And he did just that. The little glimpse he had gotten into Benjamin's life had so excited him that he was willing to make any sacrifice to enjoy such a restful control over his own existence.

Moment of Truth

Tuesday finally came and Oliver arrived at Benjamin's mansion right at 1:45 pm. Benjamin lived in a gated community and his home also had a private gate, with his initials emblazoned in gold across the structure. After maneuvering through security guards, jackrabbits crossing the golf courses, ladies crossing the street to play tennis at 2 pm, and so on, Oliver finally walked into Benjamin's house. He found him in his shorts and a hoodie. Benjamin was amusing himself with the absurdity of US politics on CNN, while working on a project he deemed top secret. He was working on the prototype for a new product he planned to launch the following year.

Benjamin welcomed Oliver and they started with some small talk. Oliver then went on to narrate his frustrations to his host, with a plea to assist him in his quest to build financial wealth. Benjamin obliged and agreed to mentor Oliver in this quest. And he began right away.

"Before we can be properly guided to go anywhere, we need to first know where we are. So, do you know your current number?" Benjamin asked.

Oliver was confused. "What number, please?"

Benjamin smiled knowingly and said: "The first step to building wealth is to first know where your wealth number currently stands. This is measured by your personal net worth. **Knowing your current net worth is the first step to building wealth**. Your personal net worth is a measure of your wealth."

Oliver knew what personal net worth was. What surprised him, however, was that despite all his studies in finance and the ideas he had obtained from other sources, he had never taken the time to calculate his personal net worth.

Sensing that his student might need further guidance on calculating his net worth, Benjamin continued: "To calculate your personal net worth is to add up all your assets and subtract all your liabilities. In simple terms, add up all the balances of your bank accounts, stock portfolio, retirement accounts, cars, houses, etc. and subtract all your debts, such as student loans, mortgages, car notes, margins, and so forth."

Oliver was certain that even though he hadn't checked his net worth, he would be pleasantly surprised at the value. He had, to the best of his knowledge, made several good financial decisions and he expected his financial number to be pretty high.

Stark Realities

Oliver rushed home and started putting together the details of his finances, as he had been taught. While on the way, Benjamin had called to inform him that there were several online tools and apps that could help in linking his bank accounts and credit balances and give him his net worth.

"These apps could also help to constantly update your number," Benjamin said. He particularly recommended an app called *Mint*.

Oliver was grateful for the tip, and immediately downloaded the app. As *Mint* computed his figures, Oliver felt ecstatic at the progress he was already making by his very first meeting with Benjamin.

Within a few hours, Oliver arrived at a number that he couldn't believe. He had to re-run the figures, again and again, but nothing changed. His net worth was a negative number; $280,734 to be exact!

Oliver was dumbfounded. He immediately became so depressed that he couldn't face his family the entire day. He couldn't believe how his American Dream had become his American Nightmare. He was actually worse off than when he was 16 years old with no debt and $277 in his custodial account that his parents had set up for him as a minor.

Oliver checked the time. It was 10:30 pm; apparently not a good time to be making phone calls. But since he had been so bothered and nothing had come out of his endless brooding, he had to call Benjamin. He had to express his frustration and ask for further guidance.

Unsurprisingly, when Oliver called Benjamin, what he got was an auto-reply text: "Sorry, can't take calls. Send SMS, if urgent." Benjamin rarely took calls after 9 pm. He liked to spend that time with his family. Oliver texted just the number, -$280,734, and followed it up with the "crying face" emoji.

Benjamin replied almost immediately, saying he wasn't surprised by Oliver's discovery. "It's a common experience," he said. The first time he had checked his own net worth, it had been a negative number, too. "Still," Benjamin added, "knowing where you currently are gives you the ability to know where you are going. **You can't improve on what you cannot measure."**

The next day, Benjamin called Oliver to inform him that both would meet at his place every Sunday, from 7 to 8 pm, so he could guide him through the path to becoming rich. Benjamin also asked Oliver to send him the breakdown of his net worth, ahead of their first meeting on Sunday. The essence was to know if Oliver had some assets that could help him build wealth quickly. Benjamin also wanted to know the exact nature of the debts that gave his mentee a negative net worth.

True to Benjamin's suspicion, Oliver's debts — as revealed by the details he sent — were all consumer loans. Mortgage, student loans, car loans, furniture loans, jewelry loans, and so forth. As he would later explain to Oliver, all debts incurred from consumption, and yes, including loans on personal mortgage, are consumer loans, which means that they have no investment value.

2
HOW DO YOU DEFINE RICH?

"To become financially-independent you must turn part of your income into capital; turn capital into enterprise; turn enterprise into profit; turn profit into investment; and turn investment into financial independence."

–Jim Rohn

Benjamin spend most of his Sundays on personal improvement. He ran longer - between five miles and a half marathon, depending on his mood. He wrote, recorded video, played music, met with friends, and read voraciously for at least an hour, among a list of other activities.

When Oliver arrived for the first coaching session, he was amazed at how rich Benjamin's life was with people. Benjamin had several people at his home, meeting with him, eating, drinking and generally having a good time. Oliver wasn't too surprised, though. He already had this understanding that Benjamin lived his life without limits. He just seemed so blessed.

Shortly after Oliver arrived, the two men went into

Benjamin's private study. It was well furnished, neat and full of artifacts, awards, books and related items. There was a large oak table with a beveled glass top that was perfectly neat. Just a notebook and a pen lay beautifully on the table.

As they began their coaching session, Benjamin looked excited and said to Oliver, "This statement may be the most important part of our entire coaching session..." Oliver listened intently for something revolutionary, as Benjamin continued: "The first rule for becoming rich in life – or even becoming successful at all - is that **you must be 'foolish' enough to pursue your goals without fear of failure. The only thing you have to fear is not fully pursuing your goals. Nothing more.**"

Oliver nodded his head, but for some reason, Benjamin didn't think that he really understood the full magnitude of the statement. So he added: "We will keep coming back to this principle throughout our sessions. This path to becoming rich will be difficult. You must develop the courage and fortitude to make tough decisions, work hard and do what others wouldn't do. It will be so tasking that you will want to lose your determination to continue. You will be tempted to feel sorry for yourself for pushing so hard. However, **you must never feel sorry for yourself. Never indulge in self-pity. No matter what the circumstances are, make a change, adjust, proceed harder but never feel sorry for yourself. Your goals are non-negotiable, your activities to achieve them are.**"

Oliver looked overwhelmed. But he managed to ask, "Would it be okay, if I copied this and placed it on my bathroom mirror?"

"I insist," Benjamin replied.

Both men smiled.

Benjamin resumed: "Now, we must define what we mean by *rich*. Interestingly, it also involves calculating a number. Since we already know your current net worth (where we are), we need to calculate your rich net worth (where we are going). To do that, we need to identify what your ideal annual income should be. **Your ideal income is an amount that you need to earn annually 'without working' or working passively to live life fully on your own terms.**"

Oliver was baffled; he had never thought about this before. A few numbers jumped to his mind - $35,000, $50 million, $1 billion, and so on. Since he couldn't make up his mind, he admitted that the question was a tricky one and eventually consoled himself with the notion that Benjamin probably had an answer and was just trying to jog his mind. So he decided to be quiet and let his host keep talking.

Benjamin, on his part, sensed Oliver's hesitation – or more precisely, confusion – and assured him that his answer didn't have to be "perfect"; all he needed was to give, as an example, what he would consider an ideal personal income. He could name any amount he considered reasonable enough to enable him to live life on his own terms. Oliver figured that $100,000 was a good number.

Benjamin concurred, and immediately proceeded to work with the figure.

He explained: "Now let's get to your rich net worth. For a simple calculation, your rich net worth is 25 times your ideal annual income. I will explain the basis of this later on, but for now, let's do the math. $100,000 times 25 gives us $2.5 million. That is your **'investable net worth'**. Congratulations, now we have a target."

A shiver ran down Oliver's spine. The number seemed daunting, but he also felt relieved that he now had a concrete target.

Benjamin continued: "Now let's discuss how we came to this multiple of 25 so that you can understand and adjust as necessary. There's a popular rule in the world of finance called 'the rule of 4 percent'. This rule says that if you spend 4 percent of your investable net worth, you should never run out of money and your net worth should keep increasing to keep up with inflation."

Oliver nodded, visibly intrigued.

"To dive deeper into this," Benjamin added, "this rule makes a few assumptions. It assumes that a well-diversified portfolio in investments, such as stocks, bonds, real estate and the likes, should conservatively return a minimum of 7 percent annually. If you factor in a relatively high inflation rate of 3 percent, your 7 percent rate of return should be able to keep up with inflation and still give you a 4 percent annual income."

Global Outlook

Benjamin gave Oliver some time to digest the last bit of information, taking time to observe his mentee's expression.

Convinced that Oliver was following his explanation,

Benjamin resumed: "Now that we have your rich net worth number, let's go over this research I saw on CNBC lately, which analyzed the perfect income for happiness around several countries. I know you just came up with a random number for your ideal annual income, so I want us to observe what other people think. This research was conducted in 2012. That means we can add an annual 3 percent inflation rate to it or take it at face value. It turns out that the lowest passive income requirement to be happy was approximately $85,000 in most of the advanced countries, the highest was approximately $276,000 and the average was approximately $161,000."

As the numbers were not too far from what Oliver had come up with, he was proud of his guess. That spurred him to speak.

"I would like to calculate the net worth needed for the annual income of all these countries. That way, if I choose to live anywhere in the world, I would still be rich."

"That's true," Benjamin said, smiling. "But you seem to have left out a very important keyword in my explanations so far – **'investable'**. I will explain why this is important shortly; but for now, I want you to calculate the various investable net worth around the globe and discuss what the numbers mean to you."

"Already doing the math," said Oliver, feeling good. "On the low end for 2012, I would need an investable net worth of $2,125,000. On average, an investable net worth of $4,025,000 and on the higher end…$6,900,000. Whew!"

"Good," said Benjamin. "Now, would you like to calculate

the 3 percent inflation rate to see what these numbers would be in today's dollars?"

Oliver was really excited to be learning so much. He blurted out in response, "Let's assume that these numbers will continually move; on the low end, I would need $3 million in net worth; on the medium end, $5 million. And if I really want to live large anywhere in the world, then I would need $10 million - for the sake of not getting stuck in the weeds."

Benjamin nodded in agreement. "I like that assumption. **$3 million, $5 million,** and **$10 million** will be our target numbers. Indeed, according to a research done by Skandia International and reported by CNBC, as of 2012, the perfect income for happiness was $161,000. You can check the report at www.cnbc.com/id/50027184."

Crucial Caveats

Benjamin continued: "I have two quick caveats for you before we end today's session. Then I will give you some homework for our next meeting. **Generally, there are three variables you need to live your life to the fullest - time, energy, and money.** Remember that our discussion is mainly about how to get the third variable, money. I must emphasize, however, that it is critical to try to hit this **ideal annual income** while the other two variables are still present to enjoy the money. There is this saying that **when you are young, you have time and energy but no money. When you are middle-aged, you have energy and money but no time. When you are old, you have time and money but no energy.**"

Benjamin allowed this to sink into Oliver, before adding:

"The trick is to try and make your investable net worth when you are middle-aged or younger. This is where this coaching differs from what a financial advisor might tell you. Anyone can become a gazillionaire by saving $300 per month for 50 years, but that puts you at age 80 or more. The average life expectancy in the United States is approximately 79. I am sure you get the picture."

Oliver nodded keenly.

"Great" Benjamin resumed. "The second caveat is the **"investable"** net worth. We did not go over the detailed calculation of net worth; my intention is to give you that as part of your homework. However, it is key to know the difference between net worth and "investable" net worth. While your primary home, cars, furniture and other properties are all part of your net worth, they are not part of your investable net worth. They are assets, not investments. **Simply put, your investable net worth would not include your primary home, cars, or other personal properties; they would only include items that are invested to generate returns for you.**"

Oliver looked bothered, but Benjamin didn't stop.

"For example, if your net worth grows to $2.8 million and your primary home is worth $1.1 million and your cars are worth a total of $100,000, we would say that your investable net worth is still only $1.6 million. You still have more work to do."

Oliver exhaled, as he pondered the two caveats. To be frank, he felt defeated. He had initially been excited to find out about the ideal annual income and net worth, but with these two new caveats of earning the annual income in a very short period and also separating his biggest assets from his investable net worth, he felt he had no chance to ever be rich and live the life that he wanted.

Benjamin noticed Oliver's disappointment and decided to cheer him up.

"Look here, Oliver," Benjamin said. "The good news is that now you know. Most people just drift throughout their entire life without having this information. The first and most critical step of any accomplishment is having a goal, a target. Now we have a target; the next step is to make it time-bound. At what age do you want to meet this target? That should be the dominant question on your mind. Settle that and let us get to work. You are in the right place, and this is the right time to do this. You can do this, Oliver."

Oliver seemed a little cheered.

"Now for your next homework…" Benjamin said. "First, let me say that this homework will set you up well for our next meeting and give you more confidence about the path through which you will attain your investable net worth in time to enjoy your ideal annual income."

Oliver listened raptly.

Benjamin deepened his voice and said, "For our next meeting, I want you to research as much as possible about people who have accomplished this goal and how they did it. Specifically, I want you to research how people under the age of 50 with over $5 million in investable net worth did it. This will be our subject population."

Oliver swiftly took notes.

Benjamin continued: "Now I understand that your ideal age might not be 50 and your investable net worth might not be $5 million, but studying this population of 50-year-olds with $5 million net worth will give us insights into what it takes to meet your definition of 'rich'. Chris Hogan, in the book, *Everyday Millionaire*, cited an extensive study of millionaires, which found that the average millionaire hits the $1 million mark at 49 years old. That's after decades of working, saving, and investing. Only 5 percent of millionaires got there in ten years or less. While this is a noteworthy accomplishment, it isn't what we are going to try and accomplish here, Oliver. Your goal is to build wealth enough to consider you rich by $5 million by the time you are 50 - preferably, a lot sooner than 50."

With that, Benjamin ended the day's coaching session.

Oliver could not contain his excitement as he drove back home. At the same time, he felt that the education system had failed him. He and Scarlett had postgraduate degrees, yet not once did they learn in school a fraction of what he was learning now. *Or could it be a conspiracy to keep the masses financially stupid?* he thought. Maybe one was expected to attend a special school, perhaps one of the best rated universities, to learn these things.

Immediately Oliver got home, he could not wait to begin his homework. He requested Scarlett to join him in his research. She gladly complied but soon began to get distracted by other engagements. Chores, school-work, homework, family, friends – all demanded her attention. In fact, while Scarlett truly wanted to help, she wasn't as interested in the project as Oliver. Oliver felt a bit discouraged but remained determined. He pored over tons of data and books, just to know what it would take to have an investable net worth of $5 million before turning 50.

Interestingly, the more Oliver read and learned, the clearer it became that he was on the wrong path; he was playing the wrong game in the wrong casino. He didn't see a path to attaining his goal in the public discourse. Everything he read kept suggesting to him to save a paltry sum out of his income so that one day when he would have been about 75 years old, he would be worth about $2 million. Essentially, it appeared that everything he read was designed to make everyone but him rich.

In the end, he concluded that the only way he could achieve his target in good time was to get additional jobs, and then save and invest more.

Brimming with eureka feeling, Oliver was eager to share this discovery with Benjamin. Unable to wait till their next scheduled meeting, he had to call him up on Friday. Benjamin listened patiently before replying: "I'm thrilled that you're making good progress. We shall see how to crystallize your discovery and ideas when we meet on Sunday."

3

THE PATH TO RICHES

"Despite a voluminous and often fervent literature on 'income distribution', the cold fact is that most income is not distributed: It is earned."

- Thomas Sowell

As evening approached on Sunday, Oliver kept glancing at the clock. He couldn't wait until it was time to start heading for his coaching session. He left some minutes past six and arrived at Benjamin's house early, excited to dig in.

After the brief exchange of pleasantries, Benjamin asked: "Do you remember what I told you the most important part of this coaching session was?" Oliver thought deeply. "Yes, the **"investable net worth"** or the **"ideal annual passive income"**

"Good," Benjamin replied. "I didn't ask that for the mere purpose of testing your memory. I just wanted the keywords in the answer reiterated for emphasis. You must also always remember that **the most important part of getting rich isn't the "what" to do, but the "will" to do it.** As I told you earlier, **you must be foolish enough to pursue your**

goals without fear of failure; the only thing you have to fear is not fully pursuing your goals. Nothing more."

Oliver indicated that he remembered clearly, and Benjamin continued:

"The reality is that most people do not really believe they can be rich. They want it but do not think it is possible - because it looks too daunting. Yet, as Henry Ford once said, whether you think you can or think you can't, you are absolutely correct. Ever heard of the story of Roger Bannister?"

Oliver replied that the name sounded familiar but he wasn't sure he knew anything about the bearer.

Benjamin came to his rescue: "I'll tell you his interesting story. You see, for centuries, the popular belief was that it was impossible for a human being to run a mile in 4 minutes. No one had ever done it and no one ever would – but that was until May 6, 1954, when Roger Bannister ran a mile in 3 minutes, 59.4 seconds. That was the first recorded time that a human being broke the 4-minute mile barrier. But then, just two months later, two runners ran the distance in under 4 minutes. Indeed, since that initial feat, over 1400 athletes are on record to have broken the barrier and it is now a common standard to break this marker. The current record stands at 3 minutes, 43.13 seconds. So, remember, **when you think you can't, then you wouldn't. When we (collectively) think we can't, then we (collectively) wouldn't."**

Oliver didn't show any sign of disagreement or inability to grasp what he had just heard. So, Benjamin added: "Now that we have that out of the way, let us break down the characteristics and statistics of the people who have attained what we are attempting to achieve and how they did it. This will give us an insight to the 'what' that we need to do."

Daunting Truth

Benjamin waited for Oliver to adjust himself as he prepared to do some more serious writing. Then, looking at him straight in the eyes, Benjamin said: "I have to admit, Oliver, that the probability of anyone becoming rich within our specified parameters is less than 1 percent. It is extremely rare to see people amass an investable net worth of $5 million on their own before they are 50. Having these coaching sessions together will certainly help, but the fact is that data is just not on our side."

Oliver was beginning to look flustered again, so Benjamin quickly added:

"See, **"the game" is rigged. The American Dream is rigged.** So, for most people working a job with a fixed salary and a W-2 income, amassing this kind of wealth is practically impossible. Are there mathematical ways of amassing such wealth on a modest salary? Yes, but realistically the data doesn't support that."

Oliver couldn't keep quiet any longer. "Why can't a person on a modest salary amass such wealth?"

Benjamin smiled. "Simple. Let's break down how they spend their income. According to several surveys, experts believe that most Americans lose approximately 50 percent of their income to taxes. Taxes of all sorts, but most notably are income taxes, property taxes, sales taxes, gasoline tax, social security tax, inflation tax and the likes. Approximately 50 percent gone! Some higher W-2 income earners lose up to between 70 percent."

Oliver's jaw dropped.

Benjamin smiled again and asked, "Do I need to continue?"

Oliver couldn't respond one way or the other, so Benjamin decided to continue.

"According to experts, most people lose another 20 percent to various fees and interests on debt, such as mortgage interest, credit card interest, car payment interest and fees and surcharges…all sorts! Now, we have an average of 70 percent of the typical wage income gone on expenses that do not help to build wealth. We haven't even gotten to lifestyle expenses such as food, clothing, vacation, dining out, and the rest. Is it any wonder that over 50 percent of Americans live from paycheck to paycheck? Unfortunately, Oliver, **the sad truth is that it is highly improbable that you will ever be rich.**"

Benjamin paused and it felt like an eternity. Actually, both men decided to be quiet, but for different reasons. Oliver was boiling inside. His stomach churned, his muscles tensed and his face twitched. He was deflated and distraught, alongside a cocktail of other indescribable emotions that he struggled with. Unable to hold himself any longer, he got up and went out. He desperately needed some fresh air.

Of course, Oliver knew that Benjamin was probably right. Yet, he wished he was back in the time when he thought being rich was still possible for anyone who tried. But then, aside from Benjamin, there was no one he knew personally who had actually made it. Everyone was always working, striving to get there but they were mostly frustrated trying to achieve this.

After some minutes, the cool breeze seemed to have worked wonders on Oliver's mind and nerves. He went in again, and Benjamin, who seemed unfazed by his reaction – as if it was expected – soon continued the session.

Success Models

"Now Oliver," Benjamin said, "Let's discuss the good news. The good news is that a significant number of people have achieved this feat of amassing an investable net worth of over $5 million before the age of 50. Let's find out about these people and how they made it."

Oliver's interest was mounting again.

Benjamin pulled out a report titled *The State of the Affluent* from a nearby shelf.

"This report is an industry intelligence report curated by CEG Worldwide and Wealth Engine," Benjamin said, pointing to the key details that he wanted to present to Oliver. "As you can see, the report defines **the Affluent** as people with investable assets of $1 million to $5 million; it defines **the Super Affluent** as people with investable assets of $5 million to $25 million; while **the Ultra Affluent** are people with investable assets of more than $25 million. We will focus primarily on **the Super Affluent** category, but we will also examine **the Ultra Affluent**. This will give us key insights into what it takes to get to these categories. As we dig deeper into this Oliver, we will now investigate what it takes to achieve this goal before we turn 50."

Oliver was beaming now. "This is getting exciting again," he gushed.

Benjamin resumed, "Today is a day of running data and statistics so we can put our attempt in context. Ever heard of the term, **framing**?"

Oliver wasn't sure.

"Framing is an alternative way of looking at a problem that should enable us to solve the problem with more ease," Benjamin said, while reaching for another publication on the shelf – *U.S. Trust Insights on Wealth and Worth*.

Flipping through the pages, Benjamin said: "This report paints a very grim picture for becoming wealthy. It says here that 782,000 or 0.6 percent of households in the U.S. have $5 million in investable assets or more. This basically means that 99.4 percent of households would not fit into our definition of rich."

"This is stunning," said Oliver.

"Also, according to the report," Benjamin said, "0.1 percent of households – that is, approximately 182,000 households - have investable assets of $10 million or greater. This number seems unusually low and paints a grim picture on the probability of becoming rich."

The two men decided to spend more time digging into different articles and resources on wealth and worth. After poring over several data and resource materials, they settled that approximately 2 percent of US households had an investable net worth of $5 million or more, and that this number equaled approximately 2.5 million households. Several research groups use different methodologies for their research. But after reviewing and aggregating the volumes of materials available to them, Benjamin and Oliver felt good with their findings. Oliver felt a lot better with this "framing" approach. In the end, they both agreed that this was a good place to end the day's session.

Oliver went home very encouraged. He was excited to share all he had learned with Scarlett, even as he kept wondering what the next coaching topic would be.

4

BEST SECRET OF THE RICH

"Don't be afraid to give up the good to go for the great."

- John D. Rockefeller

When the next Sunday eventually came, even Benjamin was eager to begin the day's discussion. As soon as Oliver arrived, there wasn't much room for small talk and pleasantries before Benjamin dived straight into *The State of the Affluent* report. He flipped to the page that explored the characteristics of the Affluent, the Super Affluent and the Ultra Affluent. In the Affluent category, 91.7 percent of the candidates were 50 years of age or older, which meant that 8.3 percent of individuals with a net worth of $1 million to $5 million were 50 years and under.

Since Benjamin wanted to simplify his presentation by restricting his focus to the Super Affluent and the Ultra Affluent, he decided to use whole numbers for his analysis. "For ease of calculation, he said, **approximately 2.5 million households in the US have $5 million in investable assets or more and approximately 15 percent of these households are 50 years or younger, which makes approximately 375,000 households. Essentially, Oliver,** we have less than .3 percent chance - .29 percent, to be exact - to achieve this feat. In other words, there is a 99.7 percent chance that we will not succeed."

Oliver sensed that Benjamin was sending a powerful message with the intensity of this coaching session. Perhaps Benjamin felt overly buoyed by the last meeting and wanted to ensure Oliver appreciated the magnitude of the task ahead of him. Oliver listened even more keenly, as Benjamin continued.

"Even though this number is disproportionate, it is good news for us, Oliver."

It was as if that was all Oliver needed to hear. He became even more resolute in his quest to be rich. Nothing would deter him now. He had realized that he had nothing to lose and that the target was achievable. He figured that he and Benjamin already had a study sample that was decent enough for them to examine.

Benjamin added: "Remember, this study is not a study of the total population but just a study of the Affluent."

Oliver could not believe what he was hearing. In fact, he seemed so close to the point of mental intoxication now. "Could you excuse me for a few minutes?" he said, as he made to get up. He needed some time alone to digest the report and really understand it.

"Sure," Benjamin replied.

"Can I take these with me?" Oliver said, reaching for *The State of the Affluent* and the *U.S. Trusts Insight on Wealth and Worth* reports. Benjamin obliged him and Oliver got a place for himself outside. Once there, he tried to extrapolate the reports to make sure what he was seeing was correct. As he read, he did some calculations and scribbled some notes in the book he brought with him. At a point, however, he seemed to get stuck; so, he went in again to see Benjamin.

"Hi, Ben, I want to make sure my calculation is correct. How many households are there in the US?"

"Approximately 128 million households," Benjamin replied.

"Thanks!"

Oliver went out again and tried to calculate the households with $10 million or more in investable assets. According to the *U.S. Trusts Insight of Wealth and Worth*, approximately 0.2 percent of households had such investable assets. This came back to approximately 256,000 households. Oliver was shocked. He checked again and the calculator gave the same result.

Oliver wondered why this wasn't taught in school. It was almost improbable for a 50-year-old or younger to attain a wealth level of $5 million or more; even more improbable was $10 million or more. At this point, even without Benjamin's prompting, **Oliver knew he had to change something in his trajectory of wealth. There was no way he was going to achieve the level of wealth he was targeting with his current job. His income trajectory had to change.**

Means of Wealth Acquisition

The *U.S. Trust Insights on Wealth and Worth* further dug into how people accumulated their wealth. Oliver's eyes lit up when he saw the pie chart showing the means by which the wealthy had accumulated their wealth, as obtained from a survey. The number one response was through earned income, followed by investment returns. Below is the list of the means, as represented in the chart:

1. Earned income: 77 percent
2. Investment returns: 59 percent
3. Employer equity, stock options: 35 percent
4. Real estate ownership/transactions: 28 percent
5. Sale of business: 11 percent
6. Inheritance/trust: 27 percent.

When Oliver got back in and showed the list to his coach, Benjamin told him: "An interesting list, isn't it? But I want you to note that even though inheritance/trust is a pretty sizable part of how the wealthy accumulate their wealth, we are going to skip it because we can't count on it."

Oliver raised his eyebrows. "I wish I had someone to inherit riches from."

"Not to worry; you will enjoy the process of accumulating wealth more than to have been bequeathed wealth," Benjamin said, giving Oliver that look that often indicated that he was about to say something even more significant. Then he dropped it: **"Income, not investment, will get you rich by 50."**

Benjamin went on to elaborate that even though investments are a key driver of wealth creation, investing typically grows wealth slowly and compounds later with time.

"Moreover, the more you have to invest from your income, the quicker you will build your investment seed. Let me make this clear, Oliver, aside from inheritance, the main drivers of wealth are the following:

1. Business ownership (self-employment)
2. Being a senior executive of a company (stock options/employer equity)
3. Financial instruments
4. Real estate transactions
5. Sale of business.

We will explore these deeper. But before then, with everything we discussed, do you have any thoughts that you want to share, Oliver?"

Benjamin liked to make sure his students were going along with him as he coached them. Oliver looked baffled but managed to say that he was increasingly seeing the need to change his occupation, so as to juice up his income.

"Exactly," said Benjamin. "However, here is another key factor of growing wealth: **you need to have an income that has the ability to grow exponentially, not linearly.**"

Benjamin again paused to see if this statement had made an impression on Oliver.

Taking the Plunge

Seizing the opportunity, Oliver said, "You mentioned earlier that **income, not investment, will make me rich by 50.** I am getting your point, but I have so many questions. For instance, how do I go about building an income that grows exponentially?"

"I know what you are thinking," Benjamin said. "You have a mortgage, student loans, a family to feed, a lifestyle to maintain, plus you have studied for several years to get your engineering degree and it's not easy to start your own Exxon Mobil overnight."

"Absolutely," Oliver said. "This is a daunting task. We have established that I need to choose to become the owner of a business (or have some sort of self-employment) that has the means of growing my income exponentially; or become a senior executive of a company or deal in financial instruments or become a real estate investor. All these require me to take a major gamble and leave my current employment. That is a non-starter for me; I have a family to feed!"

Benjamin took a deep breath and said, "Well I completely understand your predicament. Do you remember the first lesson we went over and the number one factor for becoming rich?"

"Knowing my ideal annual income, right?" Oliver said, sounding unsure. He then threw in a few other lessons he had learned from the coaching sessions.

Benjamin shook his head. "No, the number one and most

important lesson is: **you must be foolish enough to pursue your goals without fear of failure; the only thing you have to fear is not fully pursuing your goals. Nothing more.** This is not only the first rule but also the hardest. Now, let us examine a few people that have successfully made the jump and how they did it. **Success leaves clues and we can learn from these clues."**

Oliver nodded in agreement, as Benjamin continued:

"One of my favorite students is Noah Edo. Ironically, Noah was also employed as an engineer in the oil and gas industry and he had the same challenge that now confronts you. Noah was married and had two kids. He kept working and scratching but barely making progress. He just knew there had to be more. Fortunately, he was an eternal optimist. After our fourth coaching session, he came to me and said he had good news and bad news. He asked which I wanted to hear first, and I chose the good news. So, Noah said he had just received an offer from one of the largest power producing companies in the country, after having earlier applied for the job. He then proceeded to the 'bad news' which was that he was being laid off from his current job in two weeks. That, he said, would mean that he would spend at least a month without a job, while waiting to begin the new job at the power generating company".

Oliver looked enthralled by the narration, so Benjamin continued:

"Noah seemed upbeat however as he delivered this news. I asked him if he had enough funds to make it through until the new job started. He replied that normally he wouldn't

— and I must add that I wasn't surprised either; for even though Noah earned over the national average in income, he had lived from paycheck to paycheck. He however revealed that he had been paid a severance totaling his four months' salary, which came up to approximately $13,000. I exclaimed that this was good news and asked him if he was thinking what I was thinking. Noah replied that, from the way I was looking at him, he was tempted to say no. But I made it clear that this was his opportunity. It was his opportunity to strike out on his own path to becoming wealthy."

Oliver concurred and Benjamin added:

"Noah went home and called me the very next day. He said he was turning down the job with the power generating company."

Oliver looked shocked, with his mouth wide open. Benjamin continued:

"Noah decided to apply for all the credit cards that he could lay his hands on. His plan was to use this to leverage his finances. he figured that this was his chance to strike out. **He thought, 'let me give myself four months to work on my own business. If I don't succeed, I can always get another job.'** This took incredible courage from him. Noah figured he would cut his living expenses to a minimum and use his credit cards to finance his lifestyle. He figured that he could always pay the minimum balance and if in four months, he did not see any progress in his business, he would go back to the job market.

"Noah opened a home remodeling business and his first deal netted him a profit of $22,000 - enough money to pay off his credit card balance of $16,000 – and some surplus. Today, Noah is 42, has a net worth of $3.2 million and several employees and two thriving businesses. With the combination of the growth trajectory of Noah's income and his investments returns, he expects to hit the investable net worth of $5 million by the time he is 47 years old."

Benjamin turned to Oliver and asked, "Do you think this would have turned out the same if he had taken that job with the power generating company?"

Oliver could not respond, but both men had same answer.

Benjamin decided that it was time to be as direct as possible with Oliver. He knew Oliver got the message; but he was not sure if he still had the conviction of mind to pursue his goals. So, Benjamin said, "**Let me be clear so that neither of us is wasting his time. If you don't decide right now to pursue the path of self-employment or business ownership, then we are both wasting our time. Other than the super-talented athletes or trust fund babies, almost everyone that achieved this feat did so owning some sort of business. You don't amass a net worth of this magnitude by the age of 50 without the leverage of business. 75 per cent of all the Super Affluent are business owners and 91 per cent of all the Ultra Affluent are business owners. This rate goes much higher when you extrapolate those 50 and under.**"

With that, the day's session was ended.

5
PRODUCERS VERSUS CONSUMERS

"Every man is a consumer, and ought to be a producer. He is by constitution expensive, and needs to be rich."

- Ralph Waldo Emerson

"Listen, Oliver," Benjamin said, at their next session. "There are two teams in life. One team leads people to wealth and the other leads people to mediocrity. Which team do you want to be on?"

Frankly, Oliver didn't see the need for such a rhetorical question, as this. Why ask a question that had an obvious answer? What he wanted so badly now was to be rich, not to answer pointless questions. He decided not to say anything but to nod.

Benjamin seemed to get the message and continued: "Obviously, you want to be on the team that leads to wealth. That's why we are having these sessions. One of the most succinct ways I have heard someone describe the teams is by M.J. DeMarco in the book, *The Millionaire Fastlane*. The teams are **Team Producer** and **Team Consumer**. Team

Producer is the wealthy team. **It is just that plain and simple - the ones that produce get rich and the ones that consume do not. The countries that produce get rich and the countries that consume do not."**

Oliver looked a bit puzzled. "Do you mean I am not allowed to consume anything?"

"Absolutely not," Benjamin replied. **"But you are not allowed to solely consume; you must be on the producing team in one aspect of your life, and you must produce more than you consume in order to become wealthy."**

Oliver's expression was more relaxed now.

Benjamin continued: "Let's go over some examples of production and consumption. I will begin with the ten unique ones, which should help to give you clarity for the other instances of production versus consumption. So, here we go: Who is the producer and who is the consumer between an **employer** and an **employee**?"

"It is clear that when there is a job involved, the employer is the one producing the job, while the employee is the one consuming the job," Oliver blurted.

Benjamin smiled. "This is one of the most important relationships that determine your path to wealth." The path to wealth often requires leverage, especially leverage of people. In an employer/employee relationship, the employer leverages the resources and talents of the employee to create more value for himself or herself. Robert Kiyosaki in his book, *Rich Dad's Cash Flow Quadrant*, discussed the four quadrants of cash flow. The first is the employee quadrant **(you have a job)**. In this quadrant, you have no leverage of your time or of anyone's time. You are the consumer in this relationship. Even though you go to work and help in the production process to earn money, you are still the consumer of the job. Since you are the consumer and have no leverage, it is very difficult to build wealth at this stage and to build wealth rapidly is even tougher.

"The second quadrant is the self-employed quadrant **(you own a job)**. In this quadrant, you are the producer and the consumer of the job. It is slightly better than the first quadrant in which you are just the consumer. In this quadrant, you have some leverage. Even though your time is still limited, you can still determine how much money you want to make, based on how creative and resourceful you are, unlike in the employee model. Being self-employed, you can increase your per hour pay rate, based on your resourcefulness. You are in control. You can leverage tools; you can leverage contractors or employees to even help you perform some tasks in order to get more clients or customers."

Oliver nodded in agreement.

"Simply put," Benjamin continued, "the path to wealth in the cash flow quadrants begins with the self-employed quadrant. The self-employed quadrant leads to creating wealth faster than the employee quadrant; so there is a very good chance you get to reach the status of rich as we defined it above. However, the issue with the self-employed quadrant is that it rarely gives you the freedom that we discussed in the **time, money** and **energy** requirements to enjoy life. Being self-employed, we are the producer and the consumer of the employment. Consumption keeps us trapped in employment.

"The next quadrant discussed in Kiyosaki's book is the business owner quadrant **(you own a system and people work for you)**. This quadrant is the beginning of where you are the producer of the job. You can get income without having to necessarily participate personally in the day-to-day means of production. You have lots of leverage in this part of the quadrant. You have employees, tools, and resources to help you create income and wealth.

"The last part of the quadrant is the investor **(money works for you)**. This is the last and fourth quadrant. The faster you can leave the first quadrant and move to the second and ultimately reside in the third and fourth quadrants, the faster you can be rich."

Oliver appeared to have gobbled that up very quickly.

"Now," said Benjamin, "let's move to the next scenario. In **school** versus **student**, who produces and who consumes?"

"This relationship is simple to understand," Oliver replied. "Obviously, the school is the producer while the student is the consumer."

"Excellent!" Benjamin said. "However, I picked this example to emphasize how we can become the producer and not just the consumer of education. In this new age where information technology is abundant, the normal standard of education delivery has changed. Anyone can become an education provider these days. The barrier to providing education has been significantly reduced, due to the proliferation of the Internet and other means of communication."

Benjamin continued: "Let me give you an example with one of my past students. Leon was an avid reader of books and was enthralled by education. Unfortunately for him, despite his love of education, he never completed his bachelor's degree, due to several circumstances. During our sessions, he decided to compensate for not completing his bachelor's degree by becoming an education provider. I have to say that how Leon decided to go about becoming an education provider was ingenious. Leon basically turned $7,300 into millions. Leon had about $12,000 saved up. He hired a few freelance writers to write a few required courses for healthcare practitioners, he then hired a software development company to build a compliant website for learning. Since these courses were required, he figured, half the battle had been won. He hired a marketing expert and paid them a percentage of the revenue to market his courses. Voila! Leon was in a passive business in education as he has always wished for. Leon had simply become a producer of education."

Oliver concurred with a nod.

Benjamin continued: "The relationship between the landlord and the tenant is also clear. Landlords get rich while tenants get poor. In the pure sense of it, in this relationship, the landlord is the producer of real estate, while the tenant is the consumer of real estate. The more we produce real estate, the wealthier we get and the more we consume real estate, we tend to send more of our wealth to the landlord."

Oliver needed some clarification here and, as if Benjamin could tell what he was thinking, he added:

"There is a 'but' to that blanket statement, however. As previously discussed, you don't have to produce everything you consume. Yet, you must produce something, and you must produce it in excess enough to provide you with the means to cover all of your consumption."

With that sorted, Benjamin moved to the next relationship.

"Between the homebuilder and the homebuyer, who is the producer and who is the consumer?" Benjamin said, facing Oliver.

"Well," said Oliver, "when you phrase the question as such, it is clear that the home builder is the producer, and the homebuyer is the consumer. However, I had always thought homeownership built wealth?"

Benjamin looked impressed. "I am glad you asked this question," he said. "This is usually a very confusing topic for most people. But you are correct to say that in this relationship between the homebuilder and the homebuyer, the builder is the producer, and the buyer is the consumer. When you purchase a residential home to live in, you are consuming the property. The home is an asset; same as your car, TV, jewelry and so forth.

"However, generally, your home is an appreciating asset, unlike some of the other assets that depreciate over time. So, it is a good asset; but your home is not an investment, it is still an item that you are consuming."

Oliver took some time to reflect on this.

"I get it," he said at last. "The home still has to be maintained by the consumer. I have to pay the taxes, insurance and the likes. And it doesn't pay me back, until I sell it or get a loan against it.'

"Exactly," Benjamin affirmed, before continuing: "Now, let's see **writer** versus **reader**. I often use this example for illustration purposes. Reading is absolutely essential in life; however, when it comes to production and consumption, the writer is the producer of the copyright. The writer is the one making money - millions in some instances - by documenting their thoughts, opinions, experiments, biography, illustrations, activities, observations, and so on. By the way, I must quickly say here that the more we discuss these examples of producer-consumer relationships, the more you see them everywhere. In our quest to become rich, we have to make a conscious effort to become producers in one path of our life or more."

"Noted," Oliver said.

"Good," said Benjamin. "Then we can proceed to the **franchisor** and the **franchisee** relationship. This is like the homebuilder and homebuyer example. Apparently, being a franchisor and being a franchisee are both paths that lead to wealth; so, both can be considered producers. However, for this example, Oliver, I want you to see how producers think. In this relationship, the franchisor is the producer of the franchise system, while the franchisee is the consumer of the franchise system. As you can imagine here, the franchisor usually begins with one location and one site and then slowly builds a system that can be replicated and decides to sell the system to others for royalties and franchise fees. This shows how producers get their product or service to market efficiently and as a system. Is this clear enough?"

"Certainly," said Oliver.

"Alright, then," said Benjamin, "let's consider **lender** versus **borrower.**"

"This is a clear-cut one," Oliver jumped in. "The lender is the producer in this relationship and the borrower is the consumer. The lender gives the borrower the opportunity to rent money while the lender receives interest and principal repayment back."

"That's correct," said Benjamin. "However, we sometimes actually celebrate the borrower more than the lender. For instance, we have a housewarming party when a friend has just borrowed the largest amount of money in their life to buy a house. We celebrate a business owner getting approval for an SBA loan. We celebrate someone that has just leased a car…and so on. I really believe that we need to encourage ourselves to become lenders, instead of borrowers. There are several platforms that we can use to easily become lenders, just as we have several platforms that we can use to become writers and content producers."

Oliver listened attentively.

Benjamin continued: "In all honesty, Oliver, if we cannot become lenders right away, we need to at least change our culture to celebrate our friends and family when they get out of debt and not when they get into debt. For example, instead of celebrating buying a house with a loan, let's celebrate paying the house off. Let's do a housewarming party for that. Let's celebrate paying the car off, let's celebrate paying off the student loan!"

Oliver nodded in agreement but quickly asked, "How exactly can I become a lender?"

"As I already hinted," said Benjamin, "just as technology has given us several opportunities to become producers in various aspects of life, there are also opportunities to become a lender. There are several micro-lending platforms, such as Lending Club, Prosper, Kiva, and the likes. You can also buy bonds on companies, US governments and municipalities. These are all lending activities. There are also ways to become a private lender in the real estate space. I can introduce you to private lending organizations for you to work along with them."

Oliver seemed extremely interested in becoming a lender.

"I know what you're thinking," said Benjamin. But we must quickly see some more relationship scenarios. The next is **seller** versus **buyer**. In this relationship, whoever is doing the selling is the producer and whoever is doing the buying is the consumer. What this means for us is that we should often ensure that we are selling something. Is it a service or a product? If we never create and sell anything, then we are perpetually on the consumer side of wealth. As I said before, in order to build wealth, you have to be a producer. We must think as a producer. People, organizations, countries, and societies that produce more than they consume build wealth; and the opposite is true as well."

Benjamin paused to look at Oliver, and it was clear that his student was keenly following.

"Now, let's consider our last example for today - the **social media influencer** and the **social media follower** relationship. The influencer is clearly the producer here. This is actually a very powerful role. Exerting influence can be a very lucrative and powerful position to be in a relationship."

At this point, Benjamin looked straight into Oliver's eyes and said, "**Make no mistake about this; if you want to get rich the way we define rich, you have to become a producer. It is that plain and simple. You can't expect to do it solely as a consumer and plan on saving some of your earnings for 35 years, just to end up with $1.2 million at age 65. You must produce. You must move to the cash flow quadrants of self-employment, business owner and investor.** Produce for the world what you want to receive back. Be the producer of what you want, be the solution to the problem that plagues you the most. Oftentimes, the same problem plagues a lot of people. In the process of creating a solution to the problem that plagues people the most, you will become rich. Have a great week ahead!"

Oliver went home, determined to make the leap. Interestingly, it was as if Benjamin's spirit was monitoring his drive home. As soon as he arrived at his garage, even before he could get into his house, he got a call from Benjamin. Benjamin went straight to the point. "**I want you to make the decision by our next meeting what direction you want to go, and I want you to have a plan of attack.** Procrastination only gives you the opportunity to talk yourself out of what you need to do. The inevitable can't be avoided."

Benjamin usually gave his mentees one month to decide on taking the crucial leap, but he figured that Oliver needed the extra pressure.

6
BOOSTING YOUR ODDS OF GETTING RICH

"I had to make my own living and my own opportunity. But I made it! Don't sit down and wait for the opportunities to come. Get up and make them."

- Madam C.J. Walker

The following week was the most troubling for Oliver. He was at the most decisive crossroads of his life. He had to constantly affirm to himself that he could take the leap; he could pull it off. Still, he had to spend some time reflecting on his finances, his savings, his obligations to his family, and other similar concerns. He pondered which passive income he could rely on while he made the jump.

Oliver decided to engage Scarlett. He discussed with her that it would be necessary for them to tighten their belts and reduce their household expenses drastically over the next few months. Even though Oliver worked as an engineer, he had always had a flair for financial consciousness and real estate investment. So, it didn't really take too long for him to come to a decision on changing his financial outcomes. He would risk self-employment.

With his mind made up, Oliver couldn't wait for the next meeting before announcing his decision. He rang Benjamin and exclaimed, "I will do it! I will make the leap, **what do I have to lose? The path I am currently on will not get me to where I need to be. I MUST TAKE THE LEAP!"** Even Benjamin knew that with such a resolute declaration, there wasn't going to be a turning back for Oliver.

When Sunday finally came, it was Oliver who was impatient for the discussion to start. Not caring much for pleasantries, he went straight to the point. "Benjamin, I think I will start working on three businesses at a time and slowly see how things go from there."

Encouraged by Benjamin's rapt attention, Oliver continued: "I have decided to be an independent financial advisor. I have registered for a few courses that will enable me to get my license. At the same time, I will start a home construction company. This second business will start immediately, since it doesn't require a license. And, finally, I want to leverage the contacts that I have as an engineer and start a machine shop to manufacture light equipment for some of the companies in the oil and gas industries."

Oliver paused and heaved a sigh of relief. Even if Benjamin didn't approve of all his plans, he had, at least, shown that he was truly ready to act towards his financial transformation. He was proud of himself.

Benjamin, on his part, was impressed and he didn't hide it. "Congratulations," he said, stretching his hand to Oliver for a handshake. "I am extremely proud of you for making the jump. This is going to be the best decision you have made in a while. As we move forward, however, there are many lessons you still need to learn. These include focus, frugality, investing, compound interest, spending plan, and others. **Starting a business or becoming self-employed is not a silver bullet that will immediately catapult you to wealth. In other words, this is where the journey begins, not where it ends."**

Oliver rolled his eyes in resignation. "These lessons just never end," he thought to himself. But then, so be it. He was willing to undergo whatever it required to make him a multimillionaire with the decision he had taken.

Walking the Talk

There was not much to be discussed thereafter that Sunday because Oliver was eager to get to work. Starting from Monday, he started discussing with some executives of financial planning companies, while working to get his required licenses for the industry. But that was when he began to face the first set of hurdles. He realized that most of the companies were not really in the business of advising but more in the business of selling life insurance. He did not just want to sell the highest commission producing products; he wanted to really make a difference and contribute significantly to people's lives. He was disappointed in the state of the industry but he persisted and found some fee-only financial advising company. He settled in with one of them. After all, this was a pure self-employment business; you eat what you kill. He felt alive.

Simultaneously, he started having conversations with local,

small homebuilders. He went to the free classes the local builders' associations held; he saw himself making progress. He was learning a lot and chose to be disciplined. Shortly after, he ran into a couple at church that randomly asked him about a 529 plan for their kids. "Well, coincidentally, I am a financial coach," he told them. He took them on and soon got paid his first commission.

Oliver couldn't wait to get home to show Scarlett the check. "I really got paid!" he exclaimed, showing the check to Scarlett. "I have MY first check!" They were ecstatic, and that achievement further catalyzed Oliver's determination. He worked non-stop. Simultaneously, he worked on the financial coaching business, the home-building business and the metal fabrication business.

Expectedly, his very hectic schedule began to take a toll. Scarlett complained that the family never got to see him. Even when he was at home, he was constantly on phone calls or on his laptops. He missed appointments with his family and was forgetting important dates. Oliver was concerned as well, but finding a work-life balance was proving difficult with all he had to deal with.

Beginners' Manual

At the next coaching session, Oliver shared his successes and concerns with Benjamin and sought his advice. Benjamin was excited for Oliver. "This is great news," he said. "You have taken the biggest leap to a secure financial future. The challenges will always be there, but I see that you have the right attitude. You have to learn to make time for the family. Frankly, though, these next few years of your life will be the hardest, but things will ease up. In the words of Dave Ramsey, you have to live like no one else, so that you can live like no one else. "This should be your new mantra: **'I am not self-employed, I am unemployed and every day, I have to go out there and make my employment'**."

Benjamin paused for Oliver who was scribbling notes. Then, he continued:

"A lot of people make the mistake of thinking that they are self-employed and thus in full control of their own time. Unknown to them, starting and running a business or doing a self-employment business takes more commitment than having a paid job. You have to know that you are about to go on the most challenging endeavor of your life. I cannot overstate this: self-employment or business ownership is likely the most challenging thing that you will ever do. It is incredibly difficult and not for the fainthearted or the half-committed person.

"Imagine leaving a paid job for a venture that involves doing the work of a whole interdisciplinary team. You are going to be the CEO and strategist; you are going the be the salesperson; you are going to be the marketing person; you are going to be the accountant and bookkeeper; you are going to be the administrative assistant; you are going to be accounts payable assistant; you are going to be cleaner. The list goes on and on."

Benjamin paused for emphasis. He wanted to drive this idea home. Then he became even blunter: "Let us get this straight right now. **No matter how much I tell you now about how hard this journey is, it will be much harder** than whatever I say. You will never understand the heartache until you begin. Words can't do justice to it. However, the rewards are just as sweet; you cannot possibly understand how sweet the reward is until you experience it."

To Start Afresh or Buy Over?

Oliver seemed unfazed, so Benjamin continued:

"Now let's discuss how we can fast-track this wealth. Have you thought of buying a business, instead of starting one?"

Oliver was clueless about what Benjamin was referring to. He wondered if Benjamin realized that he was talking to him and not one of his other "big shot" mentees.

"Obviously not," Oliver replied. "I don't have the finances to buy a business."

"Well, let's see about that," said Benjamin. "Oliver, **according to many data sets, including from the Small Business Administration, we can infer that starting a new business has a 10 percent success rate, and only 3 percent of such businesses do succeed past 5 years. However, buying a business with systems in place has the reverse outlook - a 97 percent success rate. Which one would you rather have – a 3 percent success rate or a 97 percent success rate?"**

"This is a no-brainer," Oliver said. "I would rather have a 97 percent success rate. But that still doesn't answer the question of how I can afford to buy a business."

"Let me remind you of the first and most important rule again," Benjamin said. **"'You must be foolish enough to pursue your goals without fear of failure, the only thing you have to fear is not fully pursuing your goals. Nothing more'.** What if I told you that you could buy a business generating $1 million dollars in revenue with as little as $75,000. Would you be able to afford this?"

"Absofreakinglutely!" Oliver exclaimed. "Is this really possible?"

"Yes," Benjamin said, pulling out a listing on metal fabricating businesses. Coincidentally, this was the exact industry that Oliver was exploring to start a business. Benjamin showed him a company whose revenues were $1.2 million. This got Oliver excited.

"This company's net profit is approximately 25 percent of revenues, which is $300,000 annually," Benjamin explained.

Oliver's excitement heightened.

Benjamin continued: "This company is selling at three times the net profit, which comes up to $900,000. Now, for the kicker, Oliver. I will have my banker contact you tomorrow morning. The Small Business Administration (SBA) will let you finance the purchase of this business with 10 percent down payment. So, for $90,000, plus closing costs, you can acquire this company and have a company with systems and revenues that you can grow from day one."

Oliver couldn't contain his excitement anymore. "Now, you are talking!" he blurted out, with a fist bump in the air.

"You should have started our meetings with this, actually," he teased.

Benjamin added, "If properly negotiated, you might be able to get this business for a significant discount and even pay less than the asking $900,000 which also equates to less down payment."

Oliver was ecstatic. He wished Monday could start right away. Benjamin gave him the contact information of the business broker that was selling the business. He also gave him that of his banker for financing; his CPA and attorney, for due diligence; as well as the contacts of other consultants that could help him with the acquisition of the business.

Oliver thanked Benjamin and hurried home to Scarlett. "This was a good day," he thought to himself, "I need more days like this!"

Teething Problems

As Oliver began to act on Benjamin's advice, he noticed significant turnarounds. Although he didn't succeed in buying the initial business that Benjamin had discussed with him, he was eventually able to buy a similar business across town. This new business guaranteed more revenues, in addition to its lower cost and better terms.

Oliver was motivated to work harder and he immediately saw his income rise significantly. He was getting burnt out, however. Many months had passed by now, and it had all been about his budding businesses, coaching sessions and personal study. He hadn't taken a vacation. His mind was constantly on the next thing he could be doing.

Even more overwhelming was the fact that, while he was feeling the stress of business ownership, he didn't seem to be making much progress on his investable net worth. Sure, his income was increasing but so also was his expenditure. He had loose goals and his focus seemed to be everywhere. Soon, he began to get frustrated that he was not getting closer to becoming rich as quickly as he would have wanted.

During the next session, Oliver voiced his frustrations to Benjamin. He went on and on about how even the business ownership route didn't seem to be really for him. He had more responsibilities – there was always something to do – and without being able to take even a little break, it was becoming exhausting for him. "Sure, my income has gone up but my lifestyle has gone down. It seems I have only traded one headache for another," Oliver lamented.

To his surprise, however, Benjamin only smiled and calmly said, "Congratulations, you are making progress." He then reminded the anxious business owner what he had told him earlier, **"Starting a business or becoming self-employed is not a silver bullet that will immediately catapult you to wealth. This is where the journey begins, not where it ends."**

Benjamin continued, "Now that we have laid the foundation of true wealth-building, we must start framing the house." Benjamin had deliberately used the metaphor of home-building since Oliver was into that line of business now. His intention was to lighten up the conversation and cheer Oliver up. But his charm didn't seem to work on Oliver this time. The despairing look persisted.

"Alright, then," Benjamin said, "let's proceed to some crucial topics that should help you at this stage of your journey. These include spending plan; prioritizing saving and investments over consumption; homeownership and retirement accounts."

7
CREATING A SOLID SPENDING PLAN

"If you would be wealthy, think of saving as well as getting."
- Benjamin Franklin

"Listen carefully, Oliver," Benjamin resumed, "even though at the beginning of this coaching program, we focused on income, **the real sauce that makes the magic of wealth-building work is living below your means.** Benjamin Franklin's famous quote **'A penny saved is a penny earned'** might be the most powerful phrase in wealth-building. Money saved is more valuable than money earned. There are no two ways around this, and there is no better way of saying it. **Especially in the early days of building wealth, you must learn to practice extreme frugality."**

Appearing to have shed some of his gloominess, Oliver listened intently.

Benjamin continued: "You see, everyone hates the idea of budgeting. You hate it, and I can't pretend to like it, either. So, we may not call this budgeting; let's call it a spending plan. It is critical to create a spending plan. How are you going to spend your hard-earned money, Oliver? Would you spend it unconsciously or would you be intentional about how you spend your money?"

Since Oliver knew it was a rhetorical question, he didn't bother to answer.

"Let me ask you in a different way," Benjamin said. "Do you know how you spend your money now? For example, how much do you plan on giving to charity next month?"

Oliver looked clueless now.

"How much do you plan on saving next month? How much do you plan on spending on travel and relaxation in the next six months? How much do you plan on spending on entertainment? How much do you plan on spending on gifts? How much do you plan on investing?"

Oliver retained the clueless look, but it appeared that the lightbulb was slowly coming on in his head.

Benjamin continued: "This is why you feel that you are not making progress. You do not have a spending plan. You are living like you have made it. You are living like everyone else that is poor. Rich people have spending plans. They are intentional about how they spend. They spend a lot, but on things that matter and reflect their values. At some point in time, some rich people are so rich and have developed refined habits that they can cheat on building a spending plan, but a spending plan is non-negotiable until you attain the goal that we have set together. Once you have reached the goal of $5 million and are one of the Super Affluent, you would have developed a routine of a spending plan that you might not need to have one in writing - even though I hope you still have one. **The point is, if you want to be rich, having a spending plan is non-negotiable, plain and simple!"**

Oliver had started taking notes again. So, Benjamin paused to allow him to catch up.

Curbing Reckless Spending

After about five minutes, Benjamin resumed: "Epictetus, the Greek Stoic philosopher, once said, **'Wealth consists not in having great possessions, but in having few wants.'** I totally agree with him. As your income increases so does the temptation to increase your expenditure. It happens to everyone."

Oliver wondered whether that included Benjamin himself, since he had always seen him as a very disciplined person, immune to the weaknesses of beginners like himself.

As if reading Oliver's mind, Benjamin said, "Speaking of temptation, let me share a few secrets that I use in curbing my desires for extreme consumption."

"Oh, do you also have temptations to consume a lot?" Oliver asked.

"Absolutely," Benjamin said. "However, and even though I can consume a lot, I have found out that much of the consumption doesn't even lead to happiness. One trick I use to avoid over-consumption is to ask myself a set of questions before I make a purchase: *If no one else saw this purchase, would I still make it? Will this purchase really make me happy?* If the answer is no, I skip the purchase and move on. I also have the antidote to excessive consumption. I often try to challenge myself to see how many days I could go without spending money on consumption or any unnecessary expense. This helps me to save lots of money. As M.J. DeMarco again says, **'Every dollar saved is another freedom fighter in your army. If your money is fighting for you, your time is freed, and you break the equation of 'time for money.' Money is your army. The more you have, the more they will fight for freedom.'"**

Oliver's expression had completely changed for the better now.

"On the path to becoming rich, you must practice extreme frugality, Oliver. There aren't two ways around this. It is something you must do. The beginning days of wealth creation are too critical to spend your income as fast as you make it. Curbing your wants will be a trait that you must develop. Everything counts when you first begin your journey to accumulating wealth.

"I once read about the frugality of Warren Buffett. As you may already know, he has topped the list of the richest people in the world several times. It is said that while young Warren was building his wealth, he would often use the car of his neighbor for tasks and intentionally return the car without refilling the gas. It might sound like he was inconsiderate or even ungrateful but to Warren, every dollar wasted could be $1 million dollars, if properly invested and compound interest (which we will discuss later) got to work."

Benjamin paused to catch his breath, then continued: "I cannot honestly say that I am as frugal as Warren Buffett. In fact, I think it is a worthwhile experiment to study how frugally Warren lives his life. Personally, I think in terms of $100 expenditures. I thoroughly examine any expenditure over $100 and make sure I am getting the maximum joy out of the pleasure. As Benjamin Franklin said, 'Wealth is not his that has it, but his that enjoys it.' Every $100 I waste is akin to $350,000 I am losing in compound interest if properly invested. The thought of wasting $350,000 is less tolerable for me than the thought of wasting $100.'"

Oliver was evidently taking everything in.

"One book that really accentuates this discussion is *The Millionaire Next Door*, by Thomas J. Stanley and William D. Danko," Benjamin said, while pulling out a copy from the shelf. Even though Benjamin typically read on the 'Books' app on his iPhone, he also regularly bought hard copies of classic books for the benefit of his students.

Benjamin went over a few anecdotes from the book on how extreme frugality, coupled with a spending plan, was non-negotiable on the path of building wealth. Reading from the book, he said: "The foundation stone of wealth accumulation is defense, and this defense should be anchored by budgeting and planning." He then looked at Oliver and said, "The importance of constantly reminding yourself of the value of money earned and the need to keep it and invest it will help you to curb this syndrome of earning and losing it all. In all honesty, if we all follow this prescription of extreme frugality and savings/investing, **there should be absolutely no excuse to be 40 years old and not have** a million dollars in net worth - especially if you have been working since 18. This hinges on the power of compound interest. We only lack information.

"Really, Oliver, I don't want to belabor this point, but the importance of a spending plan and extreme frugality cannot be overstated. As we discussed in our earlier session, **even though income will make you rich, being frugal is the key to achieving financial independence.** Quite frankly, a person with a modest income and extreme frugality that invests early, consistently and wisely will certainly outpace a person with a high income and high consumption."

Benjamin paused again to allow Oliver to take notes.

"Let's use the example of the goose that lays the golden eggs, according to Aesop's fable," Benjamin resumed. "Your income is the goose. You can either consume your income today and early or you can invest your income. Let that goose become fat and productive, then you will be able to consume the golden eggs of your income forever. That will be all for today, my good friend."

Oliver got the picture and left a changed man. On getting home, he immediately began to research several spending plans tools. He found the *envelope method* of budgeting very useful. It involved prioritizing cash income to meet separate categories of household needs in physically separate envelopes. Over the next few months, Oliver and Scarlett struggled with this. Everything seemed like a need to them more than a want. He wondered if he was just that undisciplined.

One day, he called Benjamin to lament. "Benjamin, this

is tough for Scarlett and me. Despite having a detailed spending plan, we keep exceeding what we planned for in certain aspects." Oliver felt slightly ashamed, but Benjamin comforted him. "This issue is not unique to you. It is a common issue for everyone trying to build a very high income. Everything becomes a need – a private school for kids, luxury cars, golf course membership, homes in affluent neighborhoods, 33rd year birthday celebrations, and so on. Because you have the means to pay for these expenses, then everything becomes necessary."

Benjamin paused for a while and said, "I hate to recommend this but in this case, I will."

Oliver listened intently to see if he could get a pill to help him break his addiction to consumption.

Benjamin continued: "**First, never borrow money for consumption; second, categorize your spending plan into three big buckets - saving/investing, charity** and **consumption.** I feel that we are going through these topics very quickly. I wish we spent time digging deep into each item, but I also get a feeling that you are taking copious notes and really digesting this; so, I will try not to belabor each point. As we will discuss in future coaching sessions, it is critically important not to borrow money for consumption. The only consumption borrowing that I tolerate is for your personal home mortgage. I don't even tolerate borrowing money for your personal car."

Paying Yourself First

Oliver looked shocked but Benjamin didn't mind.

"On the aspect of controlling your consumption, you must learn to always pay yourself first. **Allocate a major part of your income to savings and investing. Immediately you get paid, you should remove the allocated percentage or dollar amount and move it to your brokerage account. (My preferred vehicle is some sort of index mutual funds or exchange traded funds (ETF)).** This practice gets you in the habit of consistent saving and investing. You want to save and invest automatically, right?"

Oliver agreed.

"One of my favorite books is *Success Made Simple* by Victor Lofinmakin," Benjamin continued. "This book is a must-read. It contains most of the practical anecdotes that we have discussed so far and more in big picture conceptual ideas. The book, for instance, talks of accountability and that it is impossible to hold yourself accountable. This is the challenge that you are facing, Oliver. You want to hold yourself accountable and you cannot. No one can. You have to have someone else (or a group) or a system hold you accountable."

He paused for effect and resumed: "Setting your saving and investing into an automatic withdrawal is the only way to consistently meet this part of your spending plan. This is why investing in your company's retirement plan, 401(K), 403(B), TSP and the likes, works so well. The discipline is not left to you; it is done automatically without your influence. Talking about retirement accounts, our next coaching session will focus on homeownership and retirement accounts. That's another bedrock of building wealth for the average American. This bedrock cannot be taken for granted."

Oliver digested this and couldn't wait to create his allocation. He quickly allocated 30 percent of all his income to saving and investing. He noted, also, that any excess amount over $6,000 in his checking account would be added to his savings and investments accounts. Once he set this automatic investing on, it was like magic. He saw his savings, investing and net worth grow consistently and the pace of growth grew exponentially. Oliver couldn't be happier. He was finally making progress at what he once thought was impossible!

8

HOMEOWNERSHIP AND RETIREMENT ACCOUNTS

"Owning a home is a keystone of wealth… both financial affluence and emotional security."

- Suze Orman

During the next few weeks, Oliver made considerable progress. His business grew exponentially. While he still struggled with work-life balance, he had soon started making progress in that direction too by hiring employees, including management employees. This way, he was able to free himself from some of the pressures of operating a business. He had also started seeing consistent improvement in his savings and investments rates. He, in fact, started investing in instruments that brought passive income.

It was soon time for another coaching session. Oliver got really excited about the coaching sessions these days. He now saw how much fun it was to see progress being made consistently. Benjamin was excited to see Oliver and the newfound joy he radiated. The two men chatted a bit about politics before starting to discuss homeownership and retirement accounts.

"These two factors are part of the foundation of building wealth," Benjamin began. These items are not what will cause you to meet the definition of rich that we have set for ourselves but they form the foundation that the other activities are laid upon. For most Americans, being rich will not be achieved. As we have previously realized, only approximately 2 to 2.5 percent of American households have a net worth of over $5 million and approximately 15 percent of that number are under 50 years old.

"Becoming rich is an incredible feat. However, homeownership and retirement accounts give a good runway to begin the process. They are the foundation of building wealth."

Oliver looked as if he had a question nagging at him. However, Benjamin continued. "I am sure you have heard many so-called financial gurus in the media talk about not buying a home but renting, or not investing in 401(K) because there are other investments that have higher returns than those two vehicles. The problem with their logic is that, in most cases, personal finance is more about behavior than numbers. At the level we are playing to attain wealth, it is more important to control our emotions and understand our behavior about money. We need to be aware of the returns but more importantly it is the behavior that counts the most.

"Homeownership and retirement accounts work very well because those two things are usually the biggest components of our assets when we have a net worth of $1 million or less; in some cases, it can be up to a net worth of $3 million.

Due to the effect of compound interest, these two asset/investment classes are critical because they are the classes that we can easily invest in and leave for years to allow the power of compound interest to work. For the most part, we humans get bored and one day we invest in index funds, the next day we are investing in Tesla stocks, the next day we are buying investment properties and then on to Bitcoin. These constant changes often affect our returns, allow for investments leakage (spending out of our investments on consumption), incur taxation, and have a negative effect on building wealth."

Oliver looked up again. This time he was processing all this information and he seemed to have a brainwave. "So, you mean our personal home should be the first investment we make?"

"Thank you for that question," Benjamin replied. "It shows I must repeat what I stated earlier for emphasis. **Your personal home is not an investment; it is a consumption item. However, it is an appreciating asset. It is critical to have this asset in your wealth-building portfolio but we want to keep it at a minimum. You should only purchase the right type of home that you need to be comfortable and be happy. Nothing more.** Your home is not an investment; it doesn't pay you back every month; it is an appreciating asset, but you must pay the mortgage, property taxes, insurance, maintenance etc. Buying just the right kind of home that you need is important. **The more you spend on your primary home, the less you have available to invest with.**

"Here is a revealing data about homeowners versus renters,

according to www.policygenius.com: **The average net worth of homeowners was 40 times higher than the average net worth of renters in 2019. While homeowners had a median net worth of $255,000, the median net worth of renters was only $6,300."**

Benjamin could see Oliver trying to rationalize this statistic in different ways. So, he quickly jumped in, "Don't get cute with your rationalization. I know there are several factors in play here, but the general fact remains that homeownership is one of the bedrocks of building wealth. When you purchase the right home, it enables - not hinders - you in accelerating your path to wealth."

Retirement Accounts

The two men were beginning to run out of time for that day's coaching session, so Benjamin quickly switched topics to retirement accounts. "Oliver," Benjamin said, "as we discussed earlier, one of the major hindrances to building wealth is the impact of taxes on your ability to grow your wealth. Retirement account is a great way for beginners to avoid or defer taxes on income. This is of the reasons why a retirement account is a bedrock for building wealth. Having a retirement account gives your money the runway to grow without the impact of taxes eroding your wealth along the way. In addition to this, a National Study of Millionaires by Ramsey Solutions reported that 75 percent of millionaires said that consistently investing over a long period of time was key to their financial success, hence another importance of investing in a retirement account."

He continued: "With a retirement account, we tend to keep

up with investing over a long period of time because the investing is done in the background without much effort from us. Retirement accounts are also incredible for building wealth, just as we have mentioned when we discussed homeownership. In all actuality, as we exceed $1 million to $3 million in investable assets, retirement accounts and homeownership begin to become a smaller part of our portfolio. Still, they constitute the foundation that the other wealth is built on. It is very difficult for business owners, however, to find retirement plans that they qualify for."

With that said, Benjamin gave the phone number of his financial advisor, Ike, to Oliver seek his advice. "Ike will take great care of you," Benjamin assured. "His company has options such as SEP IRA, Traditional and ROTH IRA, if you are qualified for that; but I suspect that you will not, due to your high income and other factors. However, I want to strongly encourage you to ask him to show you how to create your own company-sponsored 401(K) plans. The company-sponsored 401(K) might cost you a little extra but if properly structured could be a good retention tool for good employees. It is extremely valuable."

Oliver listened intently; he had learned to value the coaching of Benjamin. In fact, at this point, he had practically succumbed to being 'directed' by Benjamin. During their coaching session, Oliver read the key book that Benjamin recommended to him - *Success Made Simple*, by Victor Lofinmakin. Benjamin had described it as a reference guide to success, and Oliver seemed to be finding it so. The first chapter explored the "Ds" of life – 'drifting', 'driven' and 'directed'. Oliver was obviously at the "directed" stage now, and the result was the considerable progress in wealth accumulation he had been enjoying lately.

Soon after Oliver got home, he started working on homeownership and retirement accounts. He already had a personal home, but he figured that he needed to downsize. Oliver had too much money tied up in his personal home, which he felt would impact the growth of his investible asset. He however focused on properly structuring his retirement accounts. His income had grown above the threshold to contribute to the ROTH 401(K), so he decided to set up a company-sponsored 401(K) as a retention tool. However, before doing this, he learned everything he needed to know about retirement accounts. He was starting to learn so much and he wanted to be able to coach someone else in the future. **He realized that one of Benjamin's secrets to success was that he chose to help as many people as possible and coached numerous people. "The more we give, the more we get,"** Benjamin had once told him.

Going the Hard Way

When Oliver had fully optimized his retirement account for wealth-building, he immediately had a discussion with Scarlett about downsizing their home, temporarily. They needed to build wealth quickly. He explained to her that the home they lived in was the status symbol of the **'broke middle class'**, as they were overleveraged on their home. They needed a home where they could put at least 20 percent down payment; a home that was not too big for their family. It had to be just the right size and they should be able to pay it off within five years.

Oliver was beginning to think and speak like Benjamin now. He told Scarlett, "**Every extra dime we spend on a home we don't need is a dime less than we have to build wealth and get out of the rat race.**" Scarlett argued less about his decisions these days, having seen considerable improvement in their financial status. Still, she had mixed feelings about this present idea of his. Yes, she was happy because she knew it was the right thing to do, especially now that they were finally taking control of their finances. She was happy that she had a spending plan and had a grip on how she decided to spend her money. She was also happy because she knew that the downsizing was a proof that they were willing to make the necessary sacrifices to succeed, regardless of what people might say. It had dawned on her, as Oliver had often said, that **the willingness to go against the grain despite criticism is a key trait of building wealth.**

Nevertheless, Scarlett was sad that she had to leave the home that she had gotten accustomed to and all her friends might look down on her. She decided to go with her husband's idea all the same.

Oliver and Scarlett found a 1-story, 3-bedroom, 2-bathroom house that was selling at a discount and they snagged it. It turned out that Scarlett liked this home better than the big, unnecessary home they previously had. The home was cozy and brought their compact family even closer. They ended up capturing a lot of equity in this new home, which immediately increased their net worth, and they had a considerable amount of money left over to add to their investment nest egg.

So, in a nutshell, despite downsizing on their home, Scarlett and Oliver's happiness level went up. They were now feeling much more financially secure than they had ever been.

9
DEBT AND WEALTH-BUILDING

"Financial peace isn't the acquisition of stuff. It's learning to live on less than you make, so you can give money back and have money to invest. You can't win until you do this."

- Dave Ramsey

Over time, having the coaching sessions had become the highlight of Oliver and Benjamin's week. They spent time learning from each other and building each other up. It was even becoming clear to Oliver that Benjamin probably got more out of the sessions than he, the student.

They were together again for another session and Benjamin said to him, "Oliver, today, we need to discuss the issue of debt and wealth-building. This is important because our society has totally glamorized debt. So many people have come to see debt as a normal way of life. Parents begin to build their kids 'credit score' as early as age 13, so that they can be good borrowers in the future. The first thing college students get exposed to on campus are credit card companies luring them to 'free money' at ungodly interest rates. The second thing is the college itself luring them into student loans. They seem to be telling them, 'Why work?' You can just take a student loan. Don't worry; you don't have to pay it until you land that million-dollar job when you graduate. You will pay it off in no time!'"

Oliver gave Benjamin a look that indicated that he could relate to what he was saying.

Benjamin continued, "Shortly after, they're lured with a car loan, then more credit card loans, then a jewelry loan - because we all know that the 'federal law' is that you must spend at least three months' salary on an engagement ring if you want to show your fiancé that you really love her."

Oliver chuckled at this.

"Then comes a mortgage, furniture loan, Best Buy loan, Home Depot credit card, 'save 10% TODAY if you get a loan while you buy this underwear'. Then more student loans and the cycle never stops. Listen carefully, Oliver. **You must get out of consumer debt if you want to build wealth. If you want to get out a hole, the first rule is to stop digging!** Don't fool yourself thinking you can use debt wisely - you cannot. Remember that one of the rules in *Success Made Simple* is, **'You can't hold yourself accountable.'** Do not put yourself in that precarious situation of trying to play footsie with debt. Just avoid it, plain and simple. Avoid consumer debt like a plague."

Oliver's mind was by this time bubbling over with a tsunami of questions. So, he interrupted and said, "Okay, what about **"Good debt?"**

Benjamin shook his head. **"There is no 'good' consumer debt and even investment debt should be used with caution.** However, to give you a clearer picture, let us go over the debts that you consider 'good debt' and let's discuss them."

The first thing that Oliver thought of was the credit card with frequent flyer miles. So, he said, "I spend a lot of money on my business. Why shouldn't I just pay it with my credit card and pay the balance off every month and enjoy the frequent flyer miles?"

"The thinking that you are already spending money, why not get rewarded for it? is similar to saying you are already having sex, why not get rewarded for it?" Benjamin said. "Remember that credit card companies know that no one can be disciplined all the time. When you leave the option of using credit open, you will eventually succumb to the trap. **The two big financial expenses that hinder most people from building wealth are taxes and interest.** Careful attention needs to be paid to these financial expenses if you want to build wealth. These are often the two biggest line items on the expenses of most Americans."

The trouble with Keeping Debts

Sensing that Oliver still nursed some doubts, Benjamin cautioned, "Oliver, do not keep working on these mental gymnastics to justify consumer debt. Seldom would you meet a rich person that would tell you that using debt was the main cause of their wealth, especially when it is consumer debt."

He studied Oliver's expression and continued: "When you keep debt around for credit card points or because you have a low interest rate on your house, or on your car or whatever other consumer debt you have, you are hurting your chances of becoming rich for a few reasons. First, the savings you get from points on credit cards are insignificant when it comes to building wealth. When you play with fire long enough, it is bound to burn you. Just don't do it. Another reason is that when you are leveraged when you have consumer debt out there, you feel wealthier because you think you have excess cash. So you tend to spend more on unnecessary items, instead of using the excess funds to pay down debt or save and invest. This phenomenon has been studied numerous times. Whenever we feel wealthier, we spend more on consumption."

Oliver cut in, "Why should I pay off a 2.5 percent interest home mortgage when I can invest the rest and make 7 percent in the stock market?"

Benjamin smiled and said: "That is a common rationale most people use to hold on to debt for longer than they should. One of the things we mentioned about personal finance is that it is more about the behavior than the numbers. **What to do isn't the problem, doing it is. Most of us know what to do, but we don't do it. Behavior over numbers.**

"Well, back to your question, 7 is greater than 2.5, everyone knows that but almost no one will take all the excess money that they would have used to pay off the loan and invest all that money in the stock market to get 7 percent. There is always seepage. When you feel wealthier, you spend wealthier. You think of other alternative investments that you can engage in that will give you rapid wealth. You go on a more luxurious vacation. You splurge on dinner and shopping and only about 60 percent of what you saved from not paying off the mortgage and intended to invest ends up in the 'investments' column; the other 40 percent gets consumed."

Benjamin continued: "I am sure you have had instances when you had a lump sum of money with you and before you knew it, a year later, that lump sum had been cut in half and you couldn't account for it. A dollar here, a dollar there and the lump sum is gone!"

Benjamin really enjoyed this topic because it was one that most of his students often found difficult to grasp. They often had objections, so Benjamin continued to give illustrations to drive the point home.

"There are several other reasons we should always strive to pay off consumer debt," he continued with Oliver. "Still on the logic of getting 7 percent in the stock market, there are several studies that have shown that very few people get this 7 percent. Even though there is a popular saying that you should **'buy low and sell high'**, very few people end up doing this. Most people buy high and sell low. This is also due to behavior, as we discussed earlier. When the markets are crashing, most people do not have the fortitude to buy then because our instinct is when we see something going down, we believe it is going to keep going down; and, on the reverse, when we see the market going up, we jump in and buy when it is high, because also, our intuition is that when we see the market going up, it is going to keep going up. But this is not often the case."

With Oliver paying good attention, Benjamin added: "Lastly, the biggest behavioral reason that I give my students on why they should aggressively pay off their debt is the avoidance of pain. It is well documented that humans tend to have more intensity when it comes to avoidance of pain than to seek pleasure. Hence, when we are committed to paying off our consumer debt, we tend to have a greater intensity to avoid that pain and get rid of the parasitic nature of interest than the pleasure we derive from the return on investment we get from making money. It is then prudent to use that greater intensity to build wealth by focusing aggressively on crushing every consumer debt that we have and then move on to building wealth."

Power of Focus

Benjamin got up and pace the room for a few minutes. Then he said, "Let me tell you a personal story. In our early twenties, a dear friend and I decided to put this theory to test. Both of us had a huge mortgage and I decided to pay my mortgage off at the earliest possible time, while he insisted that there was no point in doing so. He said that he was going to pay the minimum and invest the rest. We had similar incomes and we started on a five-year journey of doing this. Fast forward to five years later, I had paid off my home in under two years due to intense focus."

Oliver was impressed by this, and Benjamin continued: "Quite frankly, Oliver, my total income during that period was less than my mortgage balance but somehow, I was able to pay off that mortgage. That was my first lesson on the power of focus. My friend, on the other hand, not only had a huge mortgage bill, but also suffered great losses in the stock market due to a major downturn. He withdrew the funds from the stock market to invest elsewhere because the losses seemed like they would continue forever. He maxed out his credit cards to start other business ventures. His net worth suffered significantly because of this decision not to pay off his mortgage and invest the rest.

"He has since changed his paradigm and has paid off his home. He invests regularly in index funds, real estate, and so on; and he is also a millionaire. But we both learned valuable lessons from that experiment. He now passionately instructs people on the merits of destroying all their consumer debts. **Believe it or not, you make better financial decisions when you have no consumer debt and those better financial decisions cause you to be wealthy.** Please, keep in mind that I keep referring to consumer debt."

Necessity of Leveraging

Benjamin added: "Now that you have turned into an entrepreneur, Oliver, **one of the factors that make you build wealth faster as an entrepreneur is an access to leverage, which includes people, systems and money.** Leveraging money, as an entrepreneur, for investments is useful but should be done wisely. Leveraging for real estate investments, such as commercial real estate or other business investments, could be useful as well. We will discuss the topic of leverage later in our sessions."

Benjamin paused to see if Oliver had any questions. Oliver seemed blown away at the idea of getting out of all consumer debt. He said he had always thought that being in debt was just part of the American Dream. "We are truly a debt-driven society and debt seems to allow you to enjoy a better quality of life today."

Benjamin tried to channel his inner Socrates and asked Oliver if he really thought that debt actually allowed him to enjoy a higher quality of life or fueling an early rush of getting something before he had to pay for it and then leaving him with a nasty hangover that was filled with anxiety.

Oliver thought about this deeply and said, "You are correct. When you first get the item, you are purchasing with debt, it feels good. But then comes the hard work to get the debt paid for years after the benefit of what you acquired is probably no longer relevant. Can be really infuriating."

Benjamin made Oliver promise that he would immediately begin the process of getting out of consumer debt for good. "You have to be 100 percent out of consumer debt forever," he challenged him.

Oliver didn't like to make promises he couldn't keep. He thought deep and hard about this and asked if he could take some time to ponder this before making a commitment. "Sure", Benjamin said. Oliver then asked if three weeks would be okay for him to decide. Benjamin disagreed. "I want an answer in two days or earlier," he said.

"See, Oliver," Benjamin continued. "This is a no-brainer but it is extremely critical to your ability to build wealth. As I already told you, almost none of our pentamillionaires that achieved it by their golden jubilee used consumer debt to build their wealth."

Thereafter, Benjamin continued with the coaching session as if it was a foregone conclusion that Oliver would choose the path of "no consumer debt". Benjamin knew this was achievable and with Oliver's track record of being coachable, he should eventually decide to follow this path.

The Ramsey's Model

"Ever heard of Dave Ramsey?" Benjamin asked.

"Not sure," Oliver replied.

"Dave is perhaps the best authority in the US or even the world when it comes to getting out of debt," Benjamin said. "He is a personal finance personality, radio show host, author, and businessman, whose primary focus in his broadcasts and other platforms is helping help people get out of debt. Let me make a quick confession to you Oliver, the effect of Dave Ramsey on my ability to build wealth is immense. In the beginning of my journey in building wealth, I followed his radio program religiously. I lived by the quote from his book, *The Total Money Makeover*, which says **'Focused intensity, life-or-death intensity, is required for you to reset your money-spending patterns'."**

Oliver quickly took some notes.

Benjamin continued: "On my path to building my first million in net worth, I made sure to religiously apply Dave's principles. As we discussed earlier, Oliver, getting out of debt alone will not lead you to the eventual goal; income will be your eventual tool, but you can't build wealth if you use all your income to pay finance charges from consumer debt. I am sure you have heard the phrase 'the first million is the hardest'; that is exactly what the Dave Ramsey program means to me. Once I used it to acquire my first million, the rest just came pouring in. All I had to tweak was the ability to increase the income part of the equation and the savings and investing parts as well."

Benjamin paused again to observe Oliver's reaction. Oliver had always been a good listener. He learned best by listening. And he often proved very adroit at connecting the dots and seeing the big picture. Even though Benjamin already knew this trait in Oliver, he was completely taken by surprise at his reaction this time.

"Sign me up," Oliver blurted out. "I am ready to be consumer debt-free. I do not need two days to decide. I am ready now."

Benjamin responded with another Dave Ramsey's mantra, **"Your income is your most powerful wealth-building tool, do not blow it on payments."** He added: "To wrap up today's coaching session, let us discuss Dave Ramsey's '7 Baby Steps' for getting out of debt. I printed the masterpiece from his website. It is a summary that I give to all my students. Here it is:

"Baby Step 1: Save $1000 for your starter emergency fund: *In this first step, your goal is to save $1,000 as fast as you can. Your emergency fund will cover those unexpected life events you can't plan for. And there are plenty of them. You don't want to dig a deeper hole while you're trying to work your way out of debt!*

"Baby Step 2: Pay off all debt (except the house) using the debt snowball: *Next, it's time to pay off the cars, the credit cards and the student loans. Start by listing all of your debts, except for* your mortgage. Put them in order by balance from smallest to largest—regardless of interest rate. Pay minimum payments on everything but the little one. Attack that one with a vengeance. Once it's gone, take that payment and put it toward the second-smallest debt, making minimum payments on the rest. That's what's called the debt snowball method, and you'll use it to knock out your debts one by one.

"**Baby Step 3: Save 3-6 months of expenses in a fully funded emergency fund:** You've paid off your debt! Don't slow down now. Take that money you were throwing at your debt and build a fully funded emergency fund that covers 3–6 months of your expenses. This will protect you against life's bigger surprises, like the loss of a job or your car breaking down, without slipping back into debt.

"**Baby Step 4: Invest 15% of your household income in retirement:** It's time to get serious about retirement—no matter your age. Take 15% of your gross household income and start investing it into your retirement. Start with your company's 401(k) plan and invest up to the full employer match. Then invest the rest into Roth IRAs—one for you and one for your spouse (if you're married).

"**Baby Step 5: Save for your Children's College Fund:** By this step, you've paid off all debts (except the house) and started saving for retirement. Next, it's time to save for your children's college expenses (that is, if they make it through Algebra II and Chemistry unscathed). We recommend 529 college savings plans or ESAs (Education Savings Accounts).

"**Baby Step 6: Pay off your home early:** Now, bring it all home. Baby Step 6 is the big dog! Your mortgage is the only thing between you and complete freedom from debt. Can you imagine your life with no house payment? Any extra money you can put toward your mortgage could save you tens (or even hundreds) of thousands of *dollars in interest.*

"Baby Step 7: Build wealth and give: *You know what people with no debt can do? Anything they want! The last step is the most fun. You can live and give like no one else. Keep building wealth and become outrageously generous, all while leaving an inheritance for your kids and their kids. Now that's what we call leaving a legacy!"*

After this discussion, Oliver felt some sort of relief come over him. He liked to have a plan and he could have made much more progress all along, but he never knew it. This was the plan that he ought to have been following all along. He couldn't believe that he had been stuck in Baby Step 2, despite his extremely high income. He had been in a rut and making personal finance so complicated for himself. He was now beginning to understand that personal finance was more about behavior than numbers.

Benjamin encouraged Oliver to start listening to Dave Ramsey shows in the coming months for continual motivation. "The baby steps are only the beginning," he told him.

Oliver was excited and couldn't wait to begin his baby steps. He went home and discussed this with Scarlett. Scarlett, too, was excited to be getting the new ideas. She had continued to see improvement in their quality of life in general since Oliver began the coaching sessions. She was now more excited about the future, especially now that they were both convinced that they were in control of their future. Oliver and Scarlett both swore off consumer debts forever.

10

INVESTING AND COMPOUND INTEREST

"My wealth has come from a combination of living in America, some lucky genes, and compound interest"

- Warren Buffett

A few months had passed by and Oliver and Scarlett had begun to really bask in the euphoria of their newfound financial transformation. They were implementing the ideas and lessons that they had been receiving from Benjamin – including keeping up with the Dave Ramsey's shows – and things had been working for them. They had shed their debt considerably and had seen their net worth ballooned. They had begun to invest in their retirement accounts, and were even much more focused on paying off their mortgages. They were extremely pleased with how much growth they had recorded and the prospects for the future.

Benjamin, on his part, had continued to challenge them at every step of the way. Oliver found it extremely difficult to conquer consumer debt; he was the spender in the family. He believed he needed to reward himself regularly for all his long hours and hard work. And that hadn't always made things go for him as they should.

As they met for one of their coaching sessions, Benjamin started by asking Oliver, "Do you believe in magic?" Oliver looked confused and responded, "Not really". "Well," Benjamin said. "Okay, let me ask you another question: Do you believe in miracles?" Oliver felt like this was a trick question and wondered what Benjamin was trying to achieve. He remained stoic and said, "Not really" again. "I don't really believe in magic or miracles," he declared.

Benjamin continued: "I hope I can change your mind today. We have discussed the power of compound interest briefly in previous coaching sessions, but I would like to bring it home by giving you a few illustrations on how it really works and why it is considered the "eighth wonder of the world". **On our path to building wealth, time could be our biggest friend or our biggest foe; compound interest can either work for you or against you - it depends on how you harness time and compound interest."**

Oliver listened attentively.

"Let me begin with a little personal story," Benjamin continued. Just then, he retrieved a piece of printing paper from his printer and handed it to Oliver. Oliver quickly pulled out his pen in order to take notes but Benjamin stopped him. "That won't be necessary for what I'm about to say." Benjamin then proceeded to ask him, "If you had to fold that piece of paper in your hand, how many folds do you think it would take for us to reach the moon?"

"The moon?" Oliver asked, confused.

"Yes, the moon," Benjamin affirmed.

Oliver had no idea what Benjamin was up to this time. But he decided to risk a guess. He thought to himself that the number could be five million; after all, they had been talking of $5 million. But, just then, an idea occurred to him. "Benjamin, can I ask you a question before proceeding?"

Benjamin obliged.

"What is the distance between here and the moon?" Oliver asked.

"Great, analytical question." Benjamin replied. "The distance between earth and the moon is 238,855 miles."

Oliver was glad he hadn't said 5 million. He began to think deeply on how thin the paper was and how many folds it would take to get to a mile - to start with – before talking of 238,855 miles. He thought of hazarding a guess.

"My answer is two million folds. That would be my best guess."

"Okay," said Benjamin. "But what if **I told you that you only had to fold this thin piece of paper just 42 times to get to the moon?**"

"That's impossible!" Oliver exclaimed.

"So, would you consider that magic or a miracle?" Benjamin said, grinning.

"Sure, that's more like it – either of the two."

"That is the power of time and compound interest,"

Benjamin said. "But let me give credit to where it is due. I had heard several illustrations about how compound interest worked but recently, I was sitting with my 13-year-old daughter when she thought she should amuse me with this question. She said she had learned about it from a website called www.neal.fun, not knowing that I would think of it in the aspect of compound interest. It takes only 42 folds to get to the moon. That's the power of having your money make money on prior interest or returns.

"Now if you unfold the paper by 10 folds, it is only as long as the Grand Canyon and if you unfold it by half, then it's only twice as tall as the Statue of Liberty. The power of compound interest is incredible. It is extremely important for you to start investing your extra money and start early. The earlier you start, the better of you are. You must start now. The amount you invest matters; your rate of return matters also. But the biggest factor on building wealth through investing is time. How quickly do you start, and do you invest regularly and often?

"Earlier on, we mentioned that **there's no excuse to be 40 years old and not have a million net worth if you have been working since 18, due to the power of compound interest. We only lack information. Let me also add that there's no excuse to be 50 years old and not have a net worth of $5 million dollars if you harness the power of compound interest.**"

Benjamin looked straight into Oliver's eyes and said, "You need to commit to investing regularly. Start now."

Oliver looked at Benjamin, confused. "You mean, right now?"

"Yes, right now," Benjamin confirmed. "That is the urgency of compound interest; we cannot wait for you to get home and think of not doing this. Log into your bank account online - several banks now have brokerage accounts associated with them. **This is the one magical power that anyone can harness. Whether you are a business owner or self-employed; whether you are highly paid or not, the magical powers of compound interest will work for you.**"

Oliver was intrigued, and Benjamin continued:

"The notion of the eighth wonder of the world that I mentioned earlier was actually coined by Albert Einstein. Albert Einstein once described compound interest as the eighth wonder of the world, saying that he who understands compound interest, earns it, and he who doesn't understand it, pays for it. That is how powerful one of the greatest minds in human history believed the power of compound interest to be. Oliver, I want you to pay as much attention to the power of compound interest and its ability to grow your wealth.

"But, more importantly, what most people forget is that compound interest works in both ways, when you don't apply compound interest, the inverse of compound interest destroys your wealth. When you are knee-deep in debt and you are paying compound interest to someone else, that's a big penalty to pay on the path to building your wealth."

Benjamin wanted to bring this idea of inverse of compound interest home to Oliver. He asked him to pull out his home mortgage statement from when he first purchased his home.

He asked Oliver what his interest rate was. It was a mere 4.5 percent interest. He asked Oliver to look at the statements during the first year and compare how much was going to interest versus how much was being applied to the principal payment. The number surprised Oliver, it was unbelievable.

Benjamin continued, "For a clearer illustration, let us take a loan amount of $400,000 over a typical 30-year mortgage. The first mortgage payment would only apply $526.74 towards the principal and $1500 towards interest. A whopping 3:1 ratio! Three times the amount towards interest as to principal. Do we need any more evidence of the destructive power of the inverse of compound interest if we don't have it on our side? In this example of a $400,000 loan amount on a typical 30-year mortgage, if the homeowner only made the minimum payment, the homeowner would have paid $329,619.64 in interest payments - almost as much as the principal itself. This is considering a miniscule interest rate of 4.5 percent. If the interest rate is increased to 6 percent, that would be $463,342.16 in interest payments. The power of time in compound interest is the magical sprinkle dust. The earlier, the better."

Oliver showed that he was really following Benjamin's exposition.

"That being said," Benjamin continued, "I need you to open an investment brokerage account here and now. This cannot wait any longer. You need to start investing immediately."

Oliver complied and opened a brokerage account online. He then transferred $1000 into the account. When he was done, he turned around and looked at Benjamin, as if to say,

"Now what?"

Benjamin smiled and said, "I know you are wondering what I'm up to. There is a lot to say about what just happened. I will explain it and some key issues surrounding it when we see again next week. You will understand better the tremendous significance of what has just happened."

Oliver would have wanted more explanations, but he trusted Benjamin enough to believe that he knew exactly what he was doing.

11

QUICK STEPS TO WEALTH-BUILDING

"Money makes money. And the money that makes money makes more money."

- Benjamin Franklin

When the two men met again, Benjamin began by referring to the brokerage account that Oliver had opened the previous week. He told him: "Last Sunday, you took a step that will harness one of the biggest leverages that will assist you in building wealth. We will talk about how to invest during our next coaching session. But for now, I want to highlight a few actions that you must take in order to continue to build wealth. These are actions that would work for anyone, regardless of their income. Especially for you who have built a business and have a very high income, these actions will accelerate your path to wealth."

Oliver again prepared to take notes.

Benjamin continued: "These steps were inspired by the book, *Money: Master the Game*, by Tony Robbins. These steps can be accomplished and should be taken by everyone. The author seems to condense what we have been discussing throughout the past few months into seven quick steps that we must master as we go ahead to start building our wealth.

"**Step 1: Aggressively reduce your expenditure**: As we discussed earlier, the first step to building wealth is defense. Delayed gratification is the way to wealth. Oliver, there are several investment gurus out there that will tell you that if you want a cup of coffee, go for it; you can save the rest somewhere else. If you want to eat out or splurge at a restaurant, go for it. I want to tell you today, that's not how to build wealth. In the beginning stages of wealth building, you must cut out all unnecessary expenses. There is just no way around it. If you can't say 'no' to a cup of Starbucks coffee; if you can't say 'no' to bottled water at McDonald's, instead of getting the free cup of water; if you can't say 'no' to the little things, you wouldn't be able to say 'no' to the big items.

"Starting off on defense is the best way to build wealth. Controlling your expenses is the best way to start off building wealth. This is the foundation that exposes you to all the other opportunities that you will need to build wealth. Without controlling your expenses, you wouldn't have the initial capital to build wealth by acquiring a business, investing in stocks or real estate and more. Without forcing yourself to control your expenses when your income is meager and saving is most needed, then you would not be able to discipline yourself as your income grows. One of my favorite quotes is by Benjamin Franklin who said, 'Buy what thou hast no need of and ere long thou shalt sell thy necessities.' This means that if you keep buying what you don't need, soon enough you will have to sell what you need. This is a very powerful quote for understanding the devastating effect of not being frugal. As Steve Burkholder also said, 'If you are saving, you are succeeding.'"

Benjamin paused for Oliver to catch up on his notes, then continued:

"Step 2: Aggressively save a significant portion of your income: Step two naturally flows out of step one. When you aggressively reduce your expenses, then you must aggressively save a significant portion of your income. 10 percent isn't sufficient; you must push for the most money you can save from your income. I remember during one of my coaching sessions with Paul G. After discussing the benefits of investing and establishing businesses, Paul stopped me mid-sentence, and said, 'Benjamin, I am puzzled, I understand the value of investing and all these examples that you have given of people that invested; but how did they start investing in the first place? Where did they get the capital?' This was when it dawned on me that most people do not really have the answer to this question. I told him, 'Paul, the way to build capital to begin the wealth-building journey and investing is to save money. You must save from any income that you have. That's the way most people that did not inherit their wealth did it. No one will trust you to invest their money for them without you having already demonstrated the prudence to save money. Don't think there is capital out there for you if you are a spendthrift. Reducing your expenses and aggressively saving your income is the key to begin the journey of building wealth.

"**Step 3: Invest early and often:** Once we start saving our funds, then we need to enlist the savings in the battle. The money saved needs to go and get more money for us. We need to do this for two reasons…"

Oliver's interest surged sharply at this point. He was very interested in investing. He had been hearing a lot of people talk about investing.

Benjamin continued: "As you can imagine, Oliver, if you had saved $200,000 five years ago, that could probably have bought a decent home in some parts of the United States. However, today, that would not be sufficient. So, you need to invest early to keep up with the pace of inflation. You don't want your savings to increasingly reduce its purchasing power. The other reason you need to invest is to grow your savings without your effort. When you invest, you expect to have a reasonable rate of return; you expect your investments to grow. This growth increases your net worth without too much involvement from you. As we discussed earlier, investing early and often is key. Time is the greatest power to build your investment.

"Let me give you a great illustration about the power of time on the growth of your investments. Let's say the month is January, and the day is the 1st. I have a project for you to complete for me and I can pay you in one of two different ways. The first way is I pay you $1 million on day 31 at the end of the month of January; the second way is I pay you a penny on day 1 and it doubles every day until it ends on day 31. Which option would you take, Oliver?"

Oliver thought about it. "This has got to be a trick question," he uttered.

Benjamin did not flinch; he stayed still and waited for Oliver's response. Oliver quickly did some math aloud. If he went with the penny that doubled every day, he would have $1.27 after one week, and approximately $164 after two weeks; that was halfway to the end of the project and only $164. He quickly concluded that he would go with the option of $1 million on day 31.

"I pick the first option," Oliver blurted out. "I would go with the $1 million on day 31." Benjamin continued where Oliver left off with his calculation. He said, "OK, let's continue this calculation here. By the end of the third week, you would have $20,971.51."

Oliver was feeling even prouder about his decision to pick the first option now. *Only 10 days to go, there was no way the second option could get to $1 million.*

Then Benjamin dropped the bombshell: "One week later, by day 28, you would have had $2,684,354,55; and by the end of the 31st day, the total amount would have ballooned to $21,474,836.47."

Oliver was shell-shocked. His eyeballs got so large that it seemed they would pop out of their sockets. He couldn't believe it. "This is voodoo mathematics!"

Benjamin concurred. "Exactly what I meant by the 'magical' power of compound interest. Time is the key that makes this work. Now, think about these days as years. If you invested this and it doubled every year, you would have $21,474,836.47 at the end of year 31. However, if you procrastinated and started your investment five years later you would only have

$671,088.64. The difference in procrastinating for five years would cost you $20,803,747.76.

"More interestingly, if you changed the daily pay from one penny to one dollar, you would end up becoming a billionaire in 31 days. That's a billionaire with a 'B'. A dollar doubled every day would compound to $536,870,912; that is, over $500 million at the end of 30 days and would balloon to $1,073,741,824; that is, over $1 billion at on the 31st day. This is why investing early is so critical. The earlier, the better. Start today. This is the reason I made you to open your brokerage account while you were here. We cannot afford to delay by a day. We need to start investing now and invest often. Here is the number to my financial advisor. Call him first thing in Monday morning."

Oliver expressed his appreciation and Benjamin continued:

"**Step 4: Work harder and earn more**. It's not sufficient to just invest; we must keep increasing our investment during our wealth accumulation phase. Even for self-employed people or employees, earning more money should be a continual focus of the immediate millionaire. The first part of earning more that I want to cover is industry. There is no substitute for the good old hard work. In this present world that everyone is seeking a balanced lifestyle, that balanced lifestyle cannot exist in the wealth accumulation phase."

That didn't sound well to Oliver.

Benjamin observed his countenance and said: "I wish I could tell you otherwise, but I would be wasting your time. It is a case of you picking what you want to do. There would be plenty of time for frivolous activities. However, during the wealth-building phase, you must focus on wealth-building. Let me make it a little more practical for better understanding. There are some activities that you will not have time for while building wealth; or perhaps you engage in these activities for a very short amount of time and in spurts."

Oliver braced up himself for this list of activities.

At the risk of completely losing you as a coaching student, I will rattle down a few activities. These include playing video games for hours, watching TV for hours, and staying up late night for parties 2-3 days of every week.

Oliver jumped in with a question, "What about vacations? Are those allowed?"

Benjamin liked to get Oliver involved in his own coaching; so, he asked him, "What do you think?"

Oliver said, "Vacations should be taken sparingly? Perhaps in combination with some sort of value-producing activities as well?"

"Spot on," replied Benjamin. "It is important to know that during your wealth building phase, you must focus on industry, hard work is the name of the game. Waste no time. Keeping this at the forefront of your mind is critical. Even if you are just studying, it is important to waste no time. The next item that I want to discuss with you on the path of increasing your income is leverage. This is the biggest differentiator between the employee, the self-employed, the business-owner, and the mega company founder. The difference is leverage. The more leverage you have, the greater your wealth producing capacity will be.

"There are three things you should focus on leveraging. The first is **technology** (or **systems**); the second is **people**; and the third is **money**. The main reason your income has grown exponentially is that you now have leverage. You are making more money from sources above your sole production level. Think of the amount of weight you can pull, compared to using a trailer to pull items or how far you can run, compared to using a Ferrari to travel. Leverage is the difference maker. Similarly, leverage is the difference maker in wealth-building. We all only have a limited capacity to build wealth without leverage."

Oliver then asked, "Can you give me specific ways to start building leverage in my wealth-building path?"

Benjamin decided to reverse the question. He figured that they had been at the coaching long enough to have Oliver start working on some of the thought process of the systems on his own. "What sort of leverage do you need to apply to your wealth building process?" Benjamin asked Oliver.

Oliver thought deeply and threw out a few ideas. "Perhaps I can get a business coach that can assist me in my direct business with the productive types of leverage I need for my business?"

Benjamin responded with a nod that signified agreement and for Oliver to continue.

Oliver continued, "I can get better technology to help me increase my efficiency and also the company's efficiency."

Benjamin nodded again. Oliver liked the acknowledgement; so, he continued: "Perhaps I can outsource some of the lower impact tasks that I currently do so that I can focus on higher impact tasks."

Benjamin expressed approval again and Oliver continued, "Well, I don't need any capital infusion in my current business, but I can leverage some money to purchase the building where my company is and collect the rent from all the other tenants."

Benjamin smiled, impressed. "It seems you don't need me anymore."

They both chuckled and Benjamin said, "The last thing I want to discuss on earning more is excellence. The only thing that will keep you on top of your game always is excellence. Excellence must be your motto. In everything you do, focus on excellence. This is the greatest approach you can take to your life: **In pursuit of excellence.**

"Step 5: Invest majority of your increased earnings (Do not increase your expenditure or lifestyle at the same pace of your increased income)."

Oliver continued to take copious notes. He found his new lessons on building wealth to be incredible. He wished he had known these principles earlier and more importantly he wished he had started acting on them much sooner. Nonetheless, he was committed to making these principles the guiding force of his pursuit in building wealth.

Benjamin continued: **"When you have successfully increased your income through industry, leverage and excellence, do not increase your lifestyle at the same pace of your increased income.** Several high earners make this mistake. You were tilting towards that direction at one time too. That's not strange, as I have seen several of my students fall into this trap. I was furious at one time when one of them – let's call him Parker H. - showed up at a coaching session with a $220,000 custom-ordered Mercedes Benz G-Wagon. As soon his income began to grow from following the earlier principles we discussed, Parker started to conspicuously display his new income. He wanted everyone to know that he had made it. He started dressing flamboyantly. He bought a bigger home, several cars and regularly picked up the tab for all his friends, whether they expected him to do so or not. I was extremely disappointed. It appeared that Parker, like other people, focused only on the ability to play offense, the ability to generate large income but failed at playing defense, the ability to save income."

Benjamin continued: "The trick to getting to our definition of rich lies squarely in your commitment to playing both defense and offense. As you increase your income, you must make a conscious effort to increase your savings by a significant portion of the increased income. This is very difficult to accomplish; the temptation to increase expenditure is crushing. You will see several people around you that make a fraction of your income and they appear to be living large and enjoying a higher quality of life than you. You must resist the temptation. Remember that only very few people have accomplished our definition of rich. Because they have a high income doesn't mean that they have the same goals as we do. We must remain focused and work diligently in the pursuit of our goal."

Oliver nodded in agreement and Benjamin continued:

"Now let's discuss the items that will take the biggest chunk of your income and ability to build wealth in the next step.

"**Step 6: Reduce your taxes, interest, fees and waste (including time waste)**: If you have diligently followed the plan we have been discussing and you have successfully reduced your consumption, you will be in a great place. As we discussed earlier, as your income grows exponentially, the single largest expense you will have will be taxes, followed by interest. If we are funding our lifestyle and investments with mostly debt, then interest will take a good chunk of our funds. We need to invest and build wealth and finally, fees from investment vehicles can be a great drain on our investments. More importantly, other forms of waste also crush our ability to build wealth. Waste such as not having a spending plan, not properly accounting for expenses and where your money goes, wasting too much time on the frivolous activity instead of spending it on self-improvement or industry, and so forth."

Oliver looked stunned; he had never analyzed his finances in such a manner before. He vowed to take considerable interest in the amount of taxes he paid, interest on loans, and the likes. Benjamin asked Oliver to contact his CPA to have a detailed discussion on actual tax planning, not just tax filing. He told him, "As your income continues to grow, you need to practice proactive tax planning. Without a doubt, taxes will become your greatest expense. Shouldn't you focus more time planning for it and maximizing the deductions, tax credits, and the rest within the tax code?"

Even though this was a rhetorical question, Oliver nodded in agreement and with conviction. His eyebrows furrowed in disbelief that he had never focused on this. Benjamin also gave Oliver the contact details of two separate CPAs and informed him of the importance of proactively going after this huge expense. He said to him, "The US tax code is actually written to benefit the wealthy. There are several deductions, tax credits, and so on, that will enable you to take full advantage of the tax code which wants to promote wealth-building and investing. Many small business owners are often too busy pursuing other activities that they do not give tax planning enough attention as it needs."

Oliver was grateful for the information.

Benjamin continued: "There is a great illustration that I want to share with you that underscores the devastating impact of taxes on your investments and ability to grow your wealth."

Oliver and Benjamin had been sitting in Benjamin's sunroom, but Benjamin had started walking to his private study now, and Oliver followed. When they got there, Benjamin opened up this top, left drawer, where he had kept a printed-out script from *Money: Master the Game*. Benjamin gave Oliver the printout and said, "Please read this out."

Oliver began: *"Let's try a metaphor: say you've got one dollar, and somehow, you're able to double it every year for 20 years. We all know this game. It's called compounding, right?*

After year one, you've doubled your dollar to $2.

Year two: $4.

Year three: $8.

Year four: $16.

Year five: $32.

If you had to guess, what do you think your dollar has grown to by year 20?

Don't cheat and peek ahead. Take a moment and guess.

Through the magic of compounding, in just two decades your dollar turns into (drumroll, please): $1,048,576! That's the incredible power of compounding!

As investors, we want to tap into this power. But, of course, the game is not that simple. In the real world, Caesar wants to be paid first. The tax man is looking for his piece. So, what's the impact of taxes on the same scenario? Once again, take a guess. If you're fortunate enough to pay only 33 percent in taxes per year, what do you think your dollar has now grown to after taxes in 20 years?

Again, take a moment and really guess.

Well, if the tax-free number was $1,048,576 . . . hmmm. With 33 percent tax, would that "be about $750,000? Or even $500,000?

Now let's look at the next column and see the incredible dollar-draining power when we take out money for our taxes each year before compounding—doubling our account. Assuming an annual tax rate of 33%, at the end of those same 20 years, the actual net amount you'll end up with is just over $28,000!

That's right, $28,000! A difference of over $1 million—and that doesn't even account for state taxes! In some states, such as California, New York, and New Jersey, you can expect the total to be significantly smaller still.

Sure, this dollar-doubling, dollar-draining scenario is based on returns you'll never see in the real world—but it illustrates what can happen when we neglect to consider the impact of taxes in our financial planning."

Oliver was astounded by the vast difference appropriate tax planning makes.

Benjamin resumed: "The second item we are discussing here is interest. This doesn't need an elaborate explanation. It is purely a function of how much debt you have, its corresponding interest rate and how long you keep the debt for. In this part of interest, we are discussing more of interest paid on consumption items, such as your primary home mortgage, student loans, car loans, and the likes. You can expand this also to your investment debts, so as to remain reasonably leveraged on business debt as well.

"Now, even though leverage on investments and business can bring about greater returns, they can also bring about greater risks. These risks are very real. It is difficult for our minds to compute risk. Our mind only has the ability to compute returns and not risk; so typically, when we hear someone talk of high risk/high reward, we often only hear high reward. It is easier for us to see that if we invest a certain amount of money and if the economy goes well or if the project goes well, we can anticipate a 20 percent return etc. We can calculate our potential rate of return; however, we can't predict that COVID will happen; we can't predict that a government coup will not happen in the US. In fact, there are so many unknowns in the future that represent a risk that we are unable to predict, which makes it hard for our minds to process risk."

Benjamin caught himself and said, "I digress. Let's get

back to the components of interest. Again, there are three components of interest. One is **principal borrowed.** Two is **interest rate, and** three is the **time to repay**. Our goal is to reduce all these three components as much as possible. In my opinion, the third one is the most devastating, and it is the one that most people suspect to be the least destructive. The longer you keep a balance on your debt, the more destructive it is to your long-term potential of wealth-building. Just like time is what makes compound interest work so hard for you, time on debt is akin to compound interest working against you. You don't want to go against compound interest. The longer you hold your debt, the more destructive it becomes."

Oliver listened closely.

Benjamin continued, "At the risk of losing you, let us take two instances. Suppose, Jane, Sandy and James all took a mortgage on a $300,000 property. Jane got a very low 3 percent interest rate, while Sandy and James got double the interest rate of Jane. They have a 6 percent interest rate respectively. If it took Jane the entire 30 years to pay off her mortgage at 3 percent interest rate and Sandy took 15 years to pay off her mortgage at 6 percent interest rate, Jane and Sandy would have effectively paid the same amount of interest in total dollars. If Sandy imitated Jane and took 30 years to pay the same mortgage at 6 percent interest rate, Sandy would have paid almost double the interest rate that Jane paid.

"Now James on the other hand also has a terrible 6 percent interest rate but he focused aggressively and paid off the property in seven years by being disciplined and not being wasteful. James would have paid less than half of the interest Jane paid, even though James had double the interest rate of Jane. Time is the most critical part of reducing your interest expense. **The longer you keep servicing a loan, the higher you pay on the interest.**

"The other two components of interest expense are self-explanatory. Constantly reduce the principal amount you borrow until you get to zero. When you have cut your consumer debt to zero, aggressively build on your investments and savings, so that you would not have to be tempted to go back into the consumer debt. The fastest way to build wealth is to avoid consumer debt. **If you want to consume something and you can't pay cash for it, don't do it, plain and simple.**

"Finally, if you must go into debt to fund some consumption, especially if you are in the early stages of your wealth-building journey, make sure you use the debt exceedingly sparingly and look for the debt with the least fees and the least interest rate. You want to reduce your overall cost of borrowing, as much as possible.

"Lastly on this topic are fees. Fees are what you pay to buy investments, to buy real estate, to sell real estate, to get financial advisors, to get insurance, to get some credit cards and so forth. We are bombarded with fees during several transactions…fees, fees, fees. Playing close attention to this blizzard of fees and minimizing it will go a long way in building wealth. Since fees are usually applied before putting your money to work on your investments, this drastically reduces the total return you get on investments. **One of the unseen costs of fees is also compound interest. The** cost compounds (rises exponentially) over time. If we calculated the lost compound interest on fees paid, we would be disgusted."

Benjamin pulled out an article from *Vanguard*. The Company Vanguard had been an advocate for low-cost investments for decades. The article from *Vanguard* discussed the devastating effects of costs. The articles proceeded by saying *"Imagine you have $100,000 invested. If the account earned 6% for the next 25 years and had no costs or fees, you will end up with about $430,000. If on the other hand, you paid a measly so-called 2% fees by some certain marketing gurus, after 25 years, you will have only about $260,000. This is due to the compounding effect of that 2% fees.* **A measly 2% fees you paid every year would wipe out almost 40% of your final account value. 2% doesn't sound so mall anymore, does it?"**

"Step 7: Invest conservatively and speed your way to wealth: Finally, the exciting stuff. Investments. This is where all my coaching students want to begin the coaching sessions with me. Quite frankly, when the students first come to me for coaching about getting wealthy, they are primarily thinking, *what's the next get-rich-quick scheme I can invest in to get rich overnight? What investment vehicle should I put the $25,000 I have just saved that will turn it into $25,000,000 overnight?"*

Oliver nodded slightly in concurrence.

Benjamin continued: "But they quickly realize that **income, not investing, will make you rich.** In this session, we want to discuss the **merits of conservative investments and how the combination of income generation, frugality**

and investments will assist you in accelerating your way to wealth. The first thing we need to discuss is *what is investing and what is speculating?* Oftentimes most people are speculating but think they are investing because they are speculating in financial instruments and not at the casinos. One of the most respected names in investing is Benjamin Graham, who was the mentor of Warren Buffett. Benjamin Graham said, 'An investment operation is one which, upon thorough ANALYSIS, promises safety of principal and a satisfactory return. Operations not meeting these requirements are speculative.'

"Warren Buffet once asked him the golden rule for investing and he replied, *'Rule number 1: Never lose money. Rule number 2: Don't forget rule number 1.'* These two definitions will be the bedrock of our investing principles, Oliver. The first one is investing in vehicles upon which analysis can relatively promise the safety of principal and a satisfactory rate of return.

"Burton G. Malkiel, the author of *A Random Walk Down Wall Street: The Time-Tested Strategy for Successful Investing* says, **'investing is a method of purchasing assets to gain profit in the form of reasonably predictable income (dividends, interest, or rentals) and/or appreciation over the long term. It is the definition of the time period for the investment return and the predictability of the returns that often distinguish an investment from a speculation. A speculator buys stocks hoping for a short-term gain over the next days or weeks. An investor buys stocks likely to produce a dependable future stream of cash returns and capital gains when measured over years or decades.'**

"Let's parse this out," Benjamin said to Oliver. "What sort of investments do you think these will be?" Oliver mentioned the obvious, "Real estate," then added, "real estate is a good investment option that meets this definition. Over centuries, perhaps millennia, real estate has proven to be a good investment vehicle that promises safety of principal and offers a satisfactory reasonable return."

"Spot on," Benjamin replied. "What other investment vehicle do you think can meet this definition of an investment?"

Oliver hesitated, then said, "I wanted to say stocks but I get a sense that I would be wrong if I say so."

"On the contrary, you would actually be correct if you said stocks," Benjamin countered. "Certain stocks, mutual funds, bonds and other financial instruments can actually have a reasonable expectation of safety of principal over the long term. Stocks actually have similar characteristics with real estate investments, especially if they are dividend paying stocks. We will discuss the details of the characteristics of real estate investments, stocks investments, and the likes at our next session but let us go over the general principles and guidelines for conservative investing."

Oliver concurred.

"Following the advice of Warren Buffett of never losing money," Benjamin said, "I have watched some of my previous students work so hard to generate income, sacrifice so much to save the income and they turn around and gambled it away in one speculative investment after the other. The sad thing is that they rarely notice this loss because they have incredible income to cover up for those mistakes. But these regular speculative mistakes typically have a negative effect on the growth of their wealth trajectory. Looking for the next hot tip, next penny stock that will go gangbusters etc. is not investing. Ensure that you have properly studied any investment before you make it. Even though past performance doesn't guarantee future results, if you take a deep look into the performance of an investment vehicle over a long period of time, that can give you an indication of potential performance in the future.

"Investing conservatively in what you know is very key when it comes to successful investing. You will make more in the long run by reducing your risk, chasing the big home run, investing conservatively and moving from one base to the next. Constantly look for investment opportunities that give you the opportunity to invest at a discount. This is what we call the margin of safety. Ask yourself, "If my investment analysis was 20 percent wrong, do I still preserve my capital or still make money? What is the worst-case scenario? Ask these questions about every investment opportunity."

12
WHERE TO INVEST

"It's not how much money you make, but how much money you keep, how hard it works for you, and how many generations you keep it for."

- Robert Kiyosaki

Oliver arrived at Benjamin's house with great excitement. He had seen his fortune change significantly during their coaching sessions. Benjamin was very proud of Oliver's accomplishments in such a very short time. "The future is very bright for him," Benjamin enthused.

Oliver and Scarlett continued to feel more strongly that they were in control of their investments and destiny. The anxious feeling of being always a day late and a dollar short had slowly dissipated. They now felt very financially secure and were very confident that they would become pentamillionaires, years before their 50th birthday. Oliver intended to retire early, way before his 50th birthday, so he could pursue other interests, such as skydiving, building a non-profit foundation, etc.

"Today' session will focus on where to invest," Benjamin

began. "Other than investing in education and self-improvement, which are important, there are three big buckets for investing. The buckets are, one, **financial instruments** such as stocks, bonds, CDs, annuities, and the likes; two, **real estate and mortgages**; and three, **direct business ownership**. These are the only three games in town – or, shall I say these are the predominant options for most people. There are several investment options in these three buckets, but the three main buckets cover all the dominant investment options.

"Let's begin by discussing the behavioral part of investing, then move to discuss the actual investment vehicles. Oliver, as we have previously discussed, in personal finance, behavior is perhaps more critical than numbers. According to several financial researchers, the habit of actually saving and investing is more important than the marginal rate of return from optimizing your investments and so on and so forth.

"To start this process, I want you and Scarlett to commit to an automatic saving and investing plan. Do not rely on self-discipline and self-accountability. Take the decision out of your hands. Set up a periodic automatic deduction from your income and bank account and have the funds go directly into an investment account that you will use to invest in one of the vehicles that we will discuss shortly.

In order to achieve the level of wealth we are trying to accomplish here, Oliver, you need to plan on saving and investing, at the very minimum, 20 percent of your income. I want to emphasize that this is the very minimum. Majority of my students who have gone to attain the level of wealth we are aspiring to actually practiced frugality and saved and invested approximately 50 percent of their wealth. The key here is to make this process of saving and investing an automatic or non-negotiable (or whatever you choose to call it) part of your life. It must be done without you having an option not to do it.

Financial Instruments Investment

"Now, let us start by discussing investments in financial instruments. Investing in financial instruments has been one of the most studied and published areas of investments and still there is so much disparity in opinions as to the right approach to optimizing the optimal results in this investment class. We are constantly seeing new products, new ideologies etc. on what makes the right pattern of investments in this category. There are buzz words such as life cycle funds, fundamental investors, technical investors, day traders, long-term investors, speculators, index funds, individual stocks, cryptocurrency, dividend stocks, dividend growth stocks, ETFs, etc. The list goes on and on. The bottom line, Oliver, is that we cannot cover all of the options here and quite frankly, I am not qualified to give you detailed guidance on all the options available in the financial instruments arena.

"There have been numerous studies and the consensus is that for passive investors such as you, the best approach is to invest in "no-load" (which means no sales charges or commissions), low expense fees index funds. There have been several research and experiments performed that it is virtually impossible to beat the index funds that track an entire market consistently by using other techniques in the market. Warren Buffett, one of the most respected investors of all time, once made a bet that the passive S&P 500 index fund would outperform a basket of hedge funds over a 10-year period…"

Oliver listened more attentively now.

"Warren Buffett asked the famous fund manager, Ted Seides, to pick a basket of at least five top hedge funds and he would pick the S&P 500 index. They both had a bet that the top 5 hedge funds will not beat the S&P 500 index over a period of ten years. This bet went from January 2008 to December 2017. The winner of the bet was to earn $1 million for his favorite charity organization. The result was not even close. It was so lopsided that Ted Seides threw in the towel before the end of the bet. The final result: S&P 500 gained 7.1 percent, annualized over the 10-year period for a total of 99 percent overall returns while the basket of hedge funds gained 2.2 percent annualized returns for a total of 24 percent total returns. Of course, there are various reasons why this bet was so lopsided; however, the result was clear."

Oliver seemed slightly disappointed. He had enjoyed stock picking over the years. As a business owner, he did not really enjoy passive investments; he liked to be active with all his endeavors.

Benjamin observed him but continued by saying, "I understand your predicament. It is relatively difficult to look away from the allure and seductiveness of all the various options posed by the financial markets. However let me reiterate that for a passive investor that does not work in the financial world, the best approach is to invest in a basket of index funds, or from no to low load mutual funds, with low expense ratios. This will give you a reasonable rate of return and decent diversification and asset allocation. 'The stock market is designed to transfer money from the active to the patient', Warren Buffet once said."

Diversification and Asset Allocation

At this point, Benjamin felt that they needed a little break. However, Oliver was enjoying the topic so much that he pleaded that they continued the session. Oliver asked, "What is this *diversification and asset allocation* that you've just mentioned? How important are these concepts?"

"As I said before, these are important issues," Benjamin replied. " In fact, I'd like you to meet with my investment professional to further discuss them. But first, let me give you some instructions on diversification. The good news is that if you invest in the S&P 500 index fund as discussed earlier, that will give you exposure to a good number of stocks on the US stock market. In addition, there are other index funds that you can use in balancing out your diversification. The most important aspects of you selecting any of these index funds would be to look at its track record over the last 10 years or more to ensure it beats the average. Make sure it has no load and has very low expense fee ratio (typically under .1 percent)."

Oliver asked for a break to confirm he understood everything Benjamin was telling him. He repeated the concepts to Benjamin as he confirmed what he wrote down. Benjamin confirmed and proceeded. "To conclude, let us talk about *asset allocation* a bit. Asset allocation and diversification go hand in hand. **Asset allocation** describes the percentage of your investment that you allocate to various types of investment vehicles, such as real estate, stocks, bonds, private companies etc."

As Benjamin was about to proceed with his instruction, Oliver interrupted him and asked about investment vehicles such as cryptocurrency and gold. Benjamin replied, "I specifically left those out because they are speculative. There is a school of thought that suggests that you should have a small portion of your investment portfolio in speculative vehicles, such as gold, cryptocurrency and others. This school of thought argues that these vehicles can act as hedge against inflation. I will let you decide on how you would like to proceed on that advice for that school of thought. There are too many variables in these two topics - which include your age, when you want to retire, what type of lifestyle you want to lead, how wealthy you are etc. Therefore, it is important to meet with my investment professional to discuss diversification and asset allocation."

Oliver said he would be glad to do so, as soon as possible.

Educational Investment

"Live as if you were to die tomorrow. Learn as if you were to live forever." - *Mahatma Gandhi*

Benjamin proceeded: "The next type of investment is rarely discussed in the financial world, largely because it is difficult to quantify the rate of return on it. However, this is perhaps the most important investment you can make. This investment pays the most dividends and the highest return – and it could be the least expensive as well."

Oliver listened keenly.

"This is an investment in yourself, betting on yourself; it is an investment in education and self-improvement. As a part of getting rich and wealthy, we must always be learning. Learning a new skill, a new idea, a new industry, broadening your perspective etc. *Leaders are readers* is a common saying out there."

Oliver looked puzzled. Even though he agreed with Benjamin on the importance of education, he was confused as to what type of education was required. "What should I educate myself on?" he asked.

"This is a great question," Benjamin replied. "First, you need to develop a curious mind. Always wonder how and why things work; why and how things are the way they are; and how things can be improved. Developing a curious mind is the bedrock of education. Second, you want to educate yourself on topics that are of interest to you or you want to become an authority on. The key here is to continually educate yourself and grow in the field of study. Making a deliberate decision to read daily, to pursue additional knowledge in a specific field of industry would lead you to great wealth.

"There is a paragraph from the book, *Set for Life* by Scott Trench, that I absolutely love. This paragraph has made such an impression on me that I study about real estate investing constantly and this study has catapulted my net worth significantly. I'd like to share this paragraph with you."

Oliver waited patiently while Benjamin retrieved the paragraph from his phone and gave it to him to read. The paragraph reads:

"One hour per day of study will put you at the top of your field within three years. Within five years you'll be a national authority. In seven years, you can be one of the best people in the world at what you do." A book a week roughly translates into about an hour of study a day. This is what it takes to attain an income in the top 1 percent of all Americans. (The threshold to be in the top 1 percent was $389,436 per year, according "to an Economic Policy Institute Study in 2013.1) In other words, reading and taking to heart one book per week, fifty books per year, will make you one of the best-educated, smartest, most-capable, and highest-paid professionals in your field."

After reading this, Oliver couldn't believe it was that simple to be at the top of one's field. He wondered why this wasn't public information. Benjamin assured him that even if it was widely known, it didn't mean that the majority would do it. "The information is only 20 percent of what makes this works, 80 percent of the rest is the action," Benjamin remarked. "That is where the winners are separated from the dreamers. Anyway, since we are already on the topic of my favorite investment vehicle, real estate, let us delve straight into it."

Real Estate Investment

Benjamin proceeded with a big grin. "Let us start with these two big ideas - **leverage** and **taxes**. These are the two biggest reasons why I love real estate. Once we have explored those two ideas, then we will explore the other pros and cons of real estate investment.

Once again, Oliver was all ears.

Benjamin proceeded: "Leverage is essentially debt or outside equity, or what we refer to in real estate as 'OPM'- Other People's Money. Before I continue, let me inform you, Oliver, we are only going to discuss the general ideas in this session. I will still expect you to invest in learning further on the topic of real estate investments."

Oliver agreed and Benjamin continued: "Real estate, unlike other investment vehicles, is a self-collateralized investment; hence the item you want to borrow money for is also the collateral."

Oliver looked puzzled. Benjamin could tell that Oliver wasn't quite following him and his explanation; so he decided to explain it differently.

"Let's say I came to you to borrow money to invest in my business, you would likely ask me for collateral in case my business goes belly up. Well, in real estate, the business is the property, and the collateral is the property. For example, if a new business owner walked into a bank that they wanted to borrow $500,000 to launch their business, they would be laughed out of the bank and possibly with a K-9. However, if you make a call to any mortgage broker or just go online, there would be hundreds of thousands of lenders, if not millions, standing by to lend you $500,000 to purchase an investment property."

Benjamin caught himself drifting.

"I have spent too much time on self-collateralization. Let us move to why leverage is important in real estate. Leverage helps you to increase your returns and also helps you to start to invest sooner. Suppose you had $50,000 to invest and you invested it in mutual funds. Suppose the mutual funds rose by 20 percent cumulatively in 3 years. You would have a gain of $10,000 for a total of $60,000 in 3 years with that investment. On the other hand, let's say you invested your $50,000 in real estate, however you used leverage and you bought an investment property of $500,000; you paid your $50,000 as your down payment or equity investment. For argument's sake, let's assume the property rose in value by 20 percent, just like the mutual fund, your $500,000 asset would have a gain of $100,000, which means you have made a 200 percent gain on your $50,000 investment.

"Let us even assume that, realistically, your property value only went up by 10 percent in the 3-year period, instead of the 20 percent we discussed above. A 10 percent rise in the value of the property is a gain of $50,000 - which is still a 100 percent return on your initial investment. You can see that, in the example, because of leverage, you are making 10 times the return or 5 times the return with the same investment you did in mutual funds because of the power of leverage."

Oliver paused to process the whole explanation. He wanted to make sure he had a full understanding of what Benjamin was explaining. So, he asked, "Can I paraphrase this leverage example to you to make sure I fully understand?" Benjamin obliged him. Oliver continued, "Essentially, with real estate, when I purchase a property, I can invest a portion of the value of the property as my down payment or equity investment and I control the whole value of the property. So, when there is a rise in the value of the property, it generally goes up, based on the value and not based on my current investment."

"Exactly!" Benjamin exclaimed. "You got it. Unlike investing in mutual funds - or investing in mutual funds without using options or margins."

Oliver decided to ask a question that had been bothering him. "If leverage is an advantage that is peculiar to real estate, then what if I use options and margins in the stock market? Wouldn't that erode the advantage of leverage in real estate?"

"Well," Benjamin said, "that's a great question. The answer is, while you can introduce leverage through options and margin in stocks, data suggests that the odds of losing your investment in trading with options and margins are considerably high, unless you have a very detailed knowledge of the trading industry."

Oliver nodded and Benjamin continued: "I feel that you have a decent understanding of the power of leverage in real estate now. Still, as I said, you need to learn more about this topic. For now, let us move on to the tax advantages of investing in real estate and then we will wrap it up for the day."

Tax Advantages of Real Estate

Benjamin proceeded: "In order not to bore you, we will discuss **depreciation** and **tax deferral.** I would have you meet with my CPA for the remainder of the tax advantages of investing in real estate."

Oliver was secretly happy about this. Even though he loved the topic of real estate, the numbers and details were starting to get a bit complex for him. He was a visual guy and would have loved to see the examples in writing.

Benjamin continued: "**Also known as phantom losses, depreciation is the ability to write down (reduce) the value of your real estate asset over time. The value that you write down can be deducted from your taxes.** In other words, even though the actual market value of your property has gone up over time, the IRS gives us the ability to write the value down, based on several formulas. This write-down makes a huge impact on our taxes. I mean HUGE!"

Oliver seemed shocked. "How can your market value go up and at the same time, you write down the value?"

"Exactly" Benjamin added. "This is one of the biggest benefits of real estate on your taxes. I suggest you contact my CPA first thing tomorrow morning to get further details on this topic, as it gets even more detailed when we start talking about bonus depreciation, cost segregation and the rest. In addition, the rule for depreciation changes all the time; so it would be unfair of me to go into the details with you because before I finish my explanation, the details of the rules might have changed again."

Oliver nodded and said, "However, it appears that I need

to go and look at the big idea around depreciation and real estate."

"Yes," Benjamin concurred, "but I want to add one more distinction on the topic of depreciation before we move on. **The IRS gives some depreciation advantage if you are considered an "active" real estate investor, as opposed to a "passive" investor. In addition, the IRS even gives more advantages if you are considered a real estate "professional", beyond an "active" investor or a "passive" investor.**

"So, when you contact my CPA tomorrow, discuss the topic of the current rules, as well as who qualifies as a real estate professional, active investor, passive investor and the current benefits."

Oliver agreed.

Benjamin added, "There is so much more to learn about this topic of depreciation that we can teach a full semester college course on it; but I will leave that to you to dig deeper and find out as much as possible on this topic."

Tax Deferral

"Oliver, the second issue I want to explore under this topic of tax advantages is tax deferral," Benjamin said. "This is also a very important aspect of the tax advantages of real estate."

Benjamin stomped his foot on the floor twice, startling and puzzling Oliver at the same time. "I want you to pay close attention to this," Benjamin said. Oliver looked alert.

"Let me give you an example," Benjamin continued. "Let's say you owned the 200 shares of Apple stocks worth $100,000; the stocks had appreciated by $50,000 from when you purchased it 3 years ago." Oliver looked stunned. "$100,000?", he quizzed.

"Yes," Benjamin replied. "Stay with me for a bit. Now suppose you thought Apple Company's best days were behind and you would like to trade your stocks for Tesla shares. You must sell your Apple shares in order to buy Tesla shares. Now when you sell your $100,000 shares of Apple, you must pay taxes on your $50,000 gain. These taxes can range within a myriad of numbers but for illustration's sake, let's just say between 15 to 40 percent, depending on the state that you live in and the current tax laws when you are selling. In this situation, let us assume that you paid 40 percent of your $50,000 profit in taxes, that's a whopping $20,000."

"Ouch!" Oliver yelled.

"Exactly, ouch," Benjamin agreed. "Now you only had $80,000 to re-invest in Tesla. From what we learned about compound interest earlier on, we can see how this erosion of capital we need to work for us constitutes a locust that eats away at our nest egg."

Oliver agreed. "That doesn't make a lot of sense. All I want to do is exchange my Apple shares for Tesla shares, I really don't want the money back. Why should I be forced to pay taxes and realize the gain now when all I want to do is just change investments?"

"I agree with you," said Benjamin. "However, if you had

this same situation with real estate, by using a method called like-kind exchange or 1031X for short, you can sell a property that has appreciated and buy another property without realizing the gains and without having to pay taxes on the sale, which gives you most of your gains back to keep fighting for you as your compound interest grows. Remember that the power of compound interest is when the money you made starts making money for you. Not only your principal continues to grow but the gains you have made also continue to grow."

Oliver looked flabbergasted. "Investing in real estate sure has some key tax advantages," he affirmed. "Absolutely," agreed Benjamin. "As Robert Kiyosaki famously said, *'My Rich Dad said the same thing. He says the purpose of a business is to buy real estate. Now, if you understand that, your brain will shift. But it's not about starting a business to make money. The purpose of a business is to acquire real estate, so you can use massive amounts of debt and pay no taxes.'*

"As always, I want to recommend that once you get home, Oliver, you and Scarlett have to call your CPA and find out all you can about the tax advantages of purchasing real estate. Right after that, I want you to call my real estate broker, Victor, and discuss how you can buy into commercial real estate. Make sure you also ask him about indirect ownership in commercial real estate through syndications.

Syndication is another discussion I would have loved to discuss with you on real estate; but I want you to go over that with Victor, my real estate broker directly. After you speak with him, I want you to call Kerry, my mortgage broker. Let her put you through what you will need to get leverage for acquiring your real estate portfolio."

Oliver promised to get this done immediately.

As he was about to leave, Benjamin whispered to him, **"Compound interest. Do it today. Do not wait to invest, invest and wait!"**

"He who loses money, loses much; He who loses a friend, loses much more; He who

loses faith, loses all.

- *Eleanor Roosevelt*

"Money has never made a man happy yet, nor will it. The more a man has, the more he wants. Instead of filling a vacuum, it makes one.

-*Benjamin Franklin*

CONCLUSION

What a befitting end to the story of Oliver and Scarlett. Oliver attended several more sessions with Benjamin, but at this point, the coaching sessions had become more of accountability sessions and advisory on specific challenges that Oliver encountered in life and business. Oliver could never have imagined how quick his life and family had turned around in just a few short years after he had been despondent about the direction of his future. There was no way to connect the dots forward from when he first decided to meet with Benjamin to begin on this journey. He just followed the process that Benjamin laid out, worked hard and the rest is history.

Oliver is completely debt-free. He has been able to achieve the stated goal of becoming a pentamillionaire before the age of 50. He still works hard in his business, but he and his family take at least a one-week vacation every month. He is completely at peace with the current trajectory of his financial situation and he and Scarlett are now building a foundation for his employees and his community to offer college scholarships for them. He has also launched his own coaching program as a way to pass the knowledge forward.

REFERENCES

DeMarco, M.J. (2011). *The Millionaire Fastlane*. Viperion Publishing.

Frank, Robert (2012). "The Perfect Income for Happiness? It's $161,000". www.cnbc.com/id/50027184

Hogan, Chris (2019). *Everyday Millionaire*. Ramsey Press.

Kiyosaki, Robert (2011). *Rich Dad's Cash Flow Quadrant*. Plata Publishing.

Lofinmakin, Victor (2016). *Success Made Simple*. Cornerstone Publishing.

Malkiel, Burton (2017). *A Random Walk Down Wall Street*. W. W. Norton & Company.

Stanley, Thomas J. and Danko, William D (1998). *The Millionaire Next Door*. Gallery Books.

Ramsey, Dave (2013). *The Total Money Makeover*. Thomas Nelson.

Ramsey, Dave. "The Seven Baby Steps" https://www.ramseysolutions.com/dave-ramsey-7-baby-steps

Robbins, Tony (2016). *Money: Master the Game*. Simon & Schuster.

"The State of the Affluent." https://www.cegworldwide.com/

Trench, Scott (2017). *Set for Life*. BiggerPockets.

Made in United States
Troutdale, OR
01/29/2025